Spanish Phrasebook for Law Enforcement and Social Services Professionals

Jarvis   Lebredo

Houghton Mifflin Company
Boston   New York

Director, Modern Language Programs:
    E. Kristina Baer
Development Manager: Beth Kramer
Associate Development Editor:
    Rafael Burgos-Mirabal
Editorial Assistant: Nasya Laymon
Manufacturing Manager: Florence Cadran
Associate Marketing Manager:
    Tina Crowley-Desprez

Printed in the U.S.A.

ISBN: 0-395-96310-9

123456789-EB-03 02 01 00 99

Preface

Four pocket phrasebooks now accompany the successful *Basic Spanish Grammar (BSG)* communication and career manual series. Each provides handy reference word lists to assist students of Spanish for specific career purposes and professionals who use Spanish in the workplace, reinforcing the practical approach that this program has offered to Spanish learners for the past twenty years.

The *BSG* series includes a core grammar textbook, two communication manuals (the introductory *Getting Along in Spanish* and the higher-level *Spanish for Communication*) and five career manuals: *Spanish for Business and Finance, Spanish for Medical Personnel, Spanish for Law Enforcement, Spanish for Social Services,* and *Spanish for Teachers.* When used in combination with the *BSG* grammar textbook, the career manuals teach students the basic structures of Spanish and the vocabulary pertaining to specific professions.

As their titles indicate, the phrasebooks include the terms and phrases that appear in six manuals:

> *Phrasebook for Getting Along in Spanish*
> *Spanish Phrasebook for Business, Finance, and Everyday Communication*

*Spanish Phrasebook for Medical and Social
    Services Professionals*
*Spanish Phrasebook for Law Enforcement and
    Social Services Professionals*

Since many learners of Spanish for specific
careers are English speakers, the phrasebooks
include Spanish–English and English–Spanish
listings. Designed for use in the office or in the
field, these phrasebooks will provide a
convenient resource for professionals who need a
brief, portable guide to common Spanish words
and phrases.

Abbreviations Used in This Book

adj.	adjective
adv.	adverb
coll.	colloquial
f.	feminine noun
fam.	familiar
form.	formal
inf.	infinitive
m.	masculine noun
Méx.	Mexico
pl.	plural
prep.	preposition
pron.	pronoun
sing.	singular

Spanish–English

A

a to, at, on
— **cargo de** in charge of
— **casa** home
— **cuadros** plaid
— **donde** where (to)
— **eso de** about (*with time*)
— **esta hora** at this time (hour)
— **la derecha** to the right
— **la fuerza** by force
— **la izquierda** to the left
— **la semana** weekly, per (a) week
— **la vista de** in the presence of, in front of
— **largo plazo** long term
— **lo mejor** perhaps, maybe
— **los costados** on the sides
— **mediados de mes (semana)** about the middle of the month (week)
— **medianoche** at midnight
— **menos que** unless
— **menudo** often
— **nadie le importa.** It's nobody's business.
— **partir de** at the beginning of; starting with; as of
— **pie** on foot
— **plazos** in installments, on time (payments)
— **rayas** pinstriped
— **su alcance** within reach
— **sus órdenes** at your service; any time
— **tiempo** on time; just in time
— **una cuadra de aquí** a block from here

— **veces** sometimes
— **ver...** let's see . . .
abandonar los estudios to drop out of school
abecedario (*m.*) alphabet
abierto(a) open
abogado(a) (*m., f.*) lawyer
— **defensor(a)** (*m., f.*) counsel for the defense
aborto (*m.*) abortion
abrigo (*m.*) coat
— **de piel** (*m.*) fur coat
abrir to open
— **las piernas y los brazos** to spreadeagle
absuelto(a) acquitted
abuelo(a) (*m., f.*) grandfather; grandmother
abusar to abuse
abuso sexual (*m.*) sexual abuse
acabar de (+ *inf.*) to have just (done something)
accesorio (*m.*) accessory
accidente (*m.*) accident
acción (*f.*) stock; share
aceite (*m.*) oil
acelerador (*m.*) accelerator
acento (*m.*) accent
aceptar to accept
acera (*f.*) sidewalk
acerca de about
ácido (*m.*) LSD
acné (*m.*) acne
acompañar to accompany, to go (come) with
aconsejar to advise
acordarse (o:ue) (de) to remember
acostar (o:ue) to put to bed
acostarse (o:ue) to lie down
actividad (*f.*) activity

acto (*m.*) act
actual present
actuar to act
acuerdo (*m.*) agreement
acumulador (*m.*) battery
acusación (*f.*) accusation
acusado(a) (*m., f.*) defendant
acusar to accuse
además (de) besides; in addition to
adentro inside
adicional additional
adicto(a) addicted
adiós good-bye
adjetivo (*m.*) adjective
administrador(a) (*m., f.*) administrator
adolescente (*m., f.*) adolescent, teenager
adonde where (to)
¿adónde? (to) where?
adulto(a) (*m., f.*) adult
advertencia Miranda (*f.*) Miranda Warning
afectar to affect
afeitarse to shave
afirmativo(a) affirmative
agacharse to bend down
agarrar to get hold of, to grab, to take
agencia (*f.*) agency
agente (*m., f.*) officer
agradecer to thank
agravarse to get worse, to worsen
agresión (*f.*) aggression; attack; assault
agresor(a) (*m., f.*) aggressor; assailant
Agte. (*abbreviation of* **agente**) officer
agua (*f.* but **el agua**) water
  — oxigenada (*f.*) hydrogen peroxide

aguardiente (*m.*)   a type of liquor
aguja (*f.*)   needle
agujerito (*m.*)   small hole
ahí   there
ahijado(a) (*m., f.*)   godson; goddaughter
ahogarse   to drown
ahora   at present, now
  — **mismo**   right now
  — **no**   not now, not at the present time
ahorita   at present, now, right away (*Méx.*)
ahorros (*m. pl.*)   savings
aire acondicionado (*m.*)   air conditioning
al (a + el)   to the; at the
  — **amanecer**   at dawn; at daybreak
  — **anochecer**   at dusk
  — **año**   yearly
  — **contado**   in cash
  — **cumplir... años**   on becoming (turning) . . .
    (years old)
  — **día**   a (per) day; daily; up to date
  — **día siguiente**   the next (following) day
  — **dorso**   over; on the back
  — **final**   at the end
  — **mediodía**   at midday (noon)
  — **mes**   monthly
  — **pie de la página**   at the bottom of the page
  — **rato**   a while later
alarma (*f.*)   alarm
alberca (*f.*)   swimming pool (*Méx.*)
alcanzar   to be enough
alcohol (*m.*)   alcohol
alcohólico(a)   alcoholic
Alcohólicos Anónimos   Alcoholics Anonymous
alegrarse (de)   to be glad

alejarse   to get away
alérgico(a)   allergic
alfabeto (*m.*)   alphabet
alfombra (*f.*)   rug, carpet
algo   something, anything
   ¿— **más?**   Anything else?
alguien   somebody, someone; anybody, anyone
algún, alguno(a)   some, any
   alguna vez   ever
alias (*m.*)   alias
aliento (*m.*)   breath
alimentar   to feed
alimento (*m.*)   food
allá   there
allí   there
almacenaje (*m.*)   storage
almohada (*f.*)   pillow
almuerzo (*m.*)   lunch
Aló.   Hello. (*on the telephone*) (*Puerto Rico*)
alojamiento (*m.*)   lodging
   — **y las comidas** (*m.*)   room and board
alquiler (*m.*)   rent
alto(a)   tall, high
¡Alto!   Halt!, Stop!
alucinaciones (*f. pl.*)   hallucinations
ama de casa (*f.* but **el ama**)   housewife
amamantar   to feed, to nurse
amarillo(a)   yellow
ambulancia (*f.*)   ambulance
amenaza (*f.*)   threat
amenazar   to threaten
americano(a)   American
ametralladora (*f.*)   machine gun
amigo(a) (*m., f.*)   friend

amortiguador (de ruido) (*m.*) muffler
   — de choque (*m.*) shock absorber
análisis (*m.*) test
anciano(a) (*m., f.*) elderly man, elderly woman;
   (*adj.*) old
andador (*m.*) walker
andar to go around, to walk
anillo (*m.*) ring
año (*m.*) year
   el — pasado last year
   el — próximo next year
   el — que viene next year
anoche last night
anormal abnormal
anotar to write down, to take note of
anteanoche the night before last
anteayer the day before yesterday
antecedente penal (*m.*) criminal record
anteojos (*m. pl.*) eyeglasses
anterior previous
antes (*adv.*) before
   — de anoche the night before last
   — de ayer the day before yesterday
   — de (*prep.*) before
   — de que lo interroguen before they
      question you
antibacteriano(a) antibacterial
antibiótico (*m.*) antibiotic
antidepresivo (*m.*) antidepressant
antihistamínico (*m.*) antihistamine
anual yearly
anualidad (*f.*) annuity
anular (*m.*) ring finger
apagado(a) turned out, turned off (*light*)

apagar   to turn off, to put out (*a fire*)
aparato eléctrico (*m.*)   electrical (household) appliance
aparecer   to appear
apartado postal (*m.*)   post office box
apartamento (*m.*)   apartment
apelación (*f.*)   appeal
apelar   to appeal
apellido (*m.*)   last name, surname
   — de soltera (*m.*)   maiden name
aplicar   to apply
apoyo (*m.*)   support
aprender   to learn
aprobación (*f.*)   approval
aproximadamente   approximately
aproximado(a)   approximate
apuntar   to point, to aim
aquel   that
aquello(a)   that
aquéllos(as) (*m., f.*)   those
aquí   here
   — está.   Here it is.
   — tiene   here is, here you have
área (*f.* but **el área**)   area
arete (*m.*)   earring
arma (*f.* but **el arma**)   weapon
   — blanca (*f.*)   blade
   — de fuego (*f.*)   firearm
arrancar   to start (*a car*)
arranque (*m.*)   starter
arreglar   to fix, to arrange
arreglo (*m.*)   arrangement
arrepentirse (e:ie)   to regret, to feel sorry
arrestado(a)   arrested

arrestar   to arrest
arrimar   to pull over (*a car*); to place nearby
artículo (*m.*)   article
artritis (*f.*)   arthritis
asaltante (*m., f.*)   assailant
asaltar   to assault; to mug; to hijack
asalto (*m.*)   assault; mugging; hold-up; hijacking
asegurado(a)   insured
aseguranza (f.)   insurance (*Méx.*)
asesinar   to murder
asesinato (*m.*)   murder
asesino(a) (*m., f.*)   murderer; assassin
asfixiar   to suffocate
así   like that, that way, so
   — que   so
   No es —.   It is not that way.
asiático(a)   Asian
asiento (*m.*)   seat
   — para el niño (*m.*)   child's car seat
asignado(a)   assigned
asilo de ancianos (*m.*)   home for the elderly
asistencia social (*f.*)   social services
asistir (a)   to attend
asma (*f.* but **el asma**)   asthma
atacar   to attack
ataque (*m.*)   aggression; attack; assault
   — al corazón (*m.*)   heart attack
atender (e:ie)   to take care of; to wait on
aterrorizado(a)   terrified, frightened
atrás   behind
atrasado(a)   behind, back
atravesar (e:ie)   to go through
atravesado(a)   pierced
audiencia (*f.*)   (court) hearing

audífono (*m.*)   hearing aid
aunque   although, even though
ausente   absent
auto(móvil) (*m.*)   car
autobús (*m.*)   bus
automático(a)   automatic
automovilístico(a)   car-related
autopista (*f.*)   highway
autoridad (*f.*)   authority
autorizar   to authorize, to allow
auxiliar de enfermera (*m., f.*)   nurse's aide
¡Auxilio!   Help!
avenida (*f.*)   avenue
averiguación (*f.*)   investigation
averiguar   to find out
avisar (de)   to advise, to warn, to let (someone)
   know, to inform, to give notice, to report, to
   notify
¡Ay, Dios mío!   Oh, God!, Oh, goodness
   gracious!
ayer   yesterday
ayuda (*f.*)   help, aid
   — **a familias con niños** (*f.*)   Aid to Families
      with Dependent Children (AFDC)
   — **en dinero** (*f.*)   financial assistance
ayudar   to help
azul   blue

B

babero (*m.*)   (baby's) bib
bajarse   to get out (off); to get down
bajito(a)   short (*in height*) (*Cuba*)

bajo under
— **juramento** under oath
— **los efectos (de)** under the influence (of)
bajo(a) short (*in height*); low
bajos ingresos low-income
bala (*f.*) bullet
balazo (*m.*) shot
bañadera (*f.*) bathtub
bañarse to bathe
bancarrota (*f.*) bankruptcy
banco (*m.*) bank
— **de sangre** (*m.*) blood bank
bañera (*f.*) bathtub (*Puerto Rico*)
baño (*m.*) bath, bathroom
banqueta (*f.*) sidewalk (*Méx.*)
bar (*m.*) bar
barato(a) inexpensive, cheap
barba (*f.*) beard
barbilla (*f.*) chin
barra (*f.*) bar
barrio (*m.*) neighborhood, district
barro (*m.*) mud
básico(a) basic
bastante quite, rather
bastón (*m.*) cane
basura (*f.*) trash, garbage
batería (*f.*) battery
baúl (*m.*) trunk (*of a car*) (*Puerto Rico y España*)
bebé (*m., f.*) baby
beber to drink
bebida (*f.*) drinking, drink, beverage
bebito (*m.*) baby
beca (*f.*) scholarship
beneficio (*m.*) benefit

biberón (*m.*)　baby bottle
bicicleta (*f.*)　bicycle
bien　fine, well
　—, gracias. ¿Y usted?　Fine, thank you. And
　　you?
bienes inmuebles (*m. pl.*)　real estate
bienes raíces (*m. pl.*)　real estate
bigote (*m.*)　moustache
bilingüe　bilingual
billetera (*f.*)　wallet
bizco(a)　cross-eyed
blanco(a)　white; caucasian
blusa (*f.*)　blouse
bobo (*m.*)　pacifier (*Puerto Rico*)
boca (*f.*)　mouth
　— abajo　face down
　— arriba　face up
bocina (*f.*)　horn
bofetada (*f.*)　slap
bolsa (*f.*)　purse
bolsillo (*m.*)　pocket
bolso (*m.*)　purse
bomba (*f.*)　bomb
　— de agua (*f.*)　water pump
　— de tiempo (*f.*)　time bomb
bombero(a) (*m., f.*)　firefighter
bono (*m.*)　bond
borracho(a)　drunk
bota (*f.*)　boot
botánica (*f.*)　store that sells herbal medicine
botar　to throw away
botella (*f.*)　bottle
botica (*f.*)　pharmacy, drugstore

botiquín de primeros auxilios (*m.*)   first-aid kit
botón (*m.*)   button
brazo (*m.*)   arm
breve   brief, short
bronquitis (*f.*)   bronchitis
bueno(a)   okay, fine, good; (*Méx.*) Hello. (*on the telephone*)
   Buenas noches.   Good evening., Good night.
   Buenas tardes.   Good afternoon.
   Buenos días.   Good morning., Good day.
bufanda (*f.*)   scarf
bujía (*f.*)   spark plug
buscar   to look for

C

caballo (*m.*)   heroin (*coll.*)
cabello (*m.*)   hair
cabeza (*f.*)   head
   — de familia (*m., f.*)   head of household
cabina (*f.*)   cab (*of a truck*)
cachete (*m.*)   cheek
cada   each, every
cadena (*f.*)   chain
cadera (*f.*)   hip
caerse   to fall (down)
café (*adj.*)   brown
caja (*f.*)   cash register
cajero(a) (*m., f.*)   cashier
cajuela (*f.*)   trunk (*of a car*) (*Méx.*)
calcetines (*m. pl.*)   socks
cálculos (*m. pl.*)   stones
   — en la vejiga (*m. pl.*)   bladder stones

— **en la vesícula** (*m. pl.*)   gallstones
calefacción (*f.*)   heat
calentador (*m.*)   heater
calentón (*m.*)   heater (*Méx.*)
calentura (*f.*)   fever
calibre (*m.*)   caliber
caliente   hot
calificar   to qualify
callado(a)   silent, quiet
callarse   to be quiet
   ¡Cállese!   Be quiet!, Shut up!
calle (*f.*)   street
calmante (*m.*)   pain killer, sedative
calmarse   to calm down; to relax
calvo(a)   bald
cama (*f.*)   bed
cámara de vídeo (*f.*)   video camera
cambiar   to change
   — **de trabajo**   to change jobs
   — **un cheque**   to cash a check
   —**(se) de ropa**   to change clothes
cambio (*m.*)   change
   — **de velocidad** (*m.*)   gearshift
camilla (*f.*)   stretcher
caminar   to walk
camino (*m.*)   road
camión (*m.*)   truck; bus (*Méx.*)
camioncito (*m.*)   small truck
camisa (*f.*)   shirt
camiseta (*f.*)   T-shirt
campo (*m.*)   field, country
cáncer (*m.*)   cancer
canoso(a)   gray-haired
cansado(a)   tired

cantidad (*f.*) amount, quantity
   — **fija** (*f.*) fixed amount
cantina (*f.*) bar
capa de agua (*f.*) raincoat
capacitación (*f.*) training
capacitado(a) able, trained
capítulo (*m.*) chapter
capó (*m.*) hood (*of a car*)
capucha (*f.*) hood (*on clothing*)
cara (*f.*) face
característica (*f.*) characteristic
carburador (*m.*) carburetor
cárcel (*f.*) jail
cardenal (*m.*) bruise
cardiograma (*m.*) cardiogram
carga (*f.*) burden
cargo (*m.*) position
caro(a) expensive
carretera (*f.*) highway
carril (*m.*) lane
carro (*m.*) car
   — **deportivo** (*m.*) sports car
   — **patrullero** (*m.*) patrol car
carta (*f.*) letter
cartera (*f.*) wallet, purse
casa (*f.*) house, home
   — **de Primeros Auxilios** (*f.*) House of First
     Aid
   — **de Socorro** (*f.*) House of Help
   — **para ancianos** (*f.*) home for the elderly
   — **rodante** (*f.*) mobile home
casado(a) married
casarse (con) to marry, to get married (to)
casco de seguridad (*m.*) safety (bike) helmet

casi   almost

caso (*m.*)   case

castaño(a)   brown (*eyes or hair*)

castigar   to punish

castigo corporal (*m.*)   corporal punishment

cataratas (*f. pl.*)   cataracts

catarro (*m.*)   cold

católico(a)   Catholic

causar   to cause

— **daño a**   to hurt

ceda el paso   yield (*traffic sign*)

ceja (*f.*)   eyebrow

celda (*f.*)   cell

cena (*f.*)   dinner, supper

centavo (*m.*)   cent

central   central

centro (*m.*)   downtown area

— **de cuidado de niños** (*m.*)   nursery school (*Puerto Rico*)

— **de reclusión de menores** (*m.*)   juvenile hall

cerca (de)   close (to), near

cercano(a)   close, near, nearby

cerrado(a)   closed, locked

cerradura (*f.*)   lock

cerrar (e:ie)   to close, to shut

— **con llave**   to lock

cerrojo (*m.*)   lock

— **de seguridad** (*m.*)   deadbolt

certificado (*m.*)   certificate

— **de bautismo** (*m.*)   baptismal certificate

— **de defunción** (*m.*)   death certificate

— **de depósito** (*m.*)   certificate of deposit (CD)

— **de matrimonio** (*m.*)   marriage certificate
— **de nacimiento** (*m.*)   birth certificate
cerveza (*f.*)   beer
cesantear   to fire (*from a job*)
césped (*m.*)   lawn
chamaco(a) (*m., f.*)   boy, girl (*Méx.*)
chamarra (*f.*)   jacket
chantaje (*m.*)   blackmail
chantajear   to blackmail
chapa (*f.*)   license plate
chaparro(a)   short (*Méx.*)
chaqueta (*f.*)   jacket
chavo (*m.*)   cent (*Puerto Rico*)
cheque (*m.*)   check
chequear   to check
chequera (*f.*)   checkbook (*Cuba y Puerto Rico*)
chichón (*m.*)   bump (*on the head*)
chico(a) (*m., f.*)   boy, girl
chicos (*m. pl.*)   children
chiva (*f.*)   heroin (*coll.*)
chocar   to collide, to run into, to hit
chocolate (*m.*)   hashish (*coll.*)
chofer (*m.*)   driver
choque (*m.*)   collision, crash
chupete (*m.*)   pacifier
chupón (*m.*)   pacifier (*Méx.*)
cicatriz (*f.*)   scar
ciego(a)   blind
cien(to) por ciento   one hundred percent
cierto(a)   certain
cigarrillo (*m.*)   cigarette
cine (*m.*)   (movie) theatre, movies
cinta adhesiva (*f.*)   adhesive tape
cinto (*m.*)   belt

cintura (*f.*)   waist
  al nivel de la —   waist-high
cinturón (*m.*)   belt
  — de seguridad (*m.*)   safety belt
cirujano(a) (*m., f.*)   surgeon
cita (*f.*)   appointment
ciudad (*f.*)   city
ciudadanía (*f.*)   citizenship
ciudadano(a) (*m., f.*)   citizen
claro(a)   light (*in color*)
  claro que sí   of course
clase (*f.*)   kind, type, class
clavo (*m.*)   speed (drugs) (*coll.*)
cliente(a) (*m., f.*)   customer, client
clínica (*f.*)   clinic, hospital
coartada (*f.*)   alibi
cobrar   to charge, to collect, to get paid
  — un cheque   to cash a check
coca (*f.*)   cocaine (*coll.*)
  — cocinada (*f.*)   crack cocaine (*coll.*)
cocaína (*f.*)   cocaine
coche (*m.*)   car
cochecito (*m.*)   baby carriage
cocina (*f.*)   kitchen, stove
cocinar   to cook
cocinero(a) (*m., f.*)   cook
código postal (*m.*)   zip code, postal code (*Méx.*)
codo (*m.*)   elbow
coger   to get hold of, to grab, to take
cognado (*m.*)   cognate
cojo(a)   one-legged; lame
cólico (*m.*)   colic
colitis (*f.*)   colitis
collar (*m.*)   necklace

colocar to place, to put

colonia (*f.*) neighborhood, district (*Méx.*)

color (*m.*) color

colorado(a) red

comadre (*f.*) godmother or mother (*in relation to each other*)

combustible (*m.*) fuel

comedor (*m.*) dining room

comenzar (e:ie) to begin, to commence

comienza la autopista freeway begins (*traffic sign*)

comer to eat

cometer to commit; to perpetrate

comida (*f.*) food, meal

comidita de bebé (*f.*) baby food

comisaría (*f.*) police station

comisión (*f.*) commission

¿cómo? how?

   ¿— es? What does he/she/you look like?

   ¿— está Ud.? How are you?

   ¡—no! Certainly!, Gladly!, Sure!

   ¿— se escribe... ? How do you spell . . . ?

como about, approximately

   — de as, like, since, being that

cómoda (*f.*) chest of drawers

compadre (*m.*) godfather or father (*in relation to each other*)

compañero(a) (*m., f.*) pal, peer, buddy, companion

   — de clase (*m., f.*) classmate

comparecer to appear

   — ante un juez to appear in court

compasión (*f.*) compassion

compensación obrera (*f.*)   worker's compensation

completar   to complete

completo(a)   complete

complexión (*f.*)   build

complicación (*f.*)   complication

cómplice (*m., f.*)   accomplice

comportarse   to behave

comprar   to buy

comprender   to understand

comprobante (*m.*)   receipt

computadora (*f.*)   computer

común   common

comunicar   to communicate

con   with

— **cuidado**   carefully

— **él**   with him

— **ella**   with her

— **frecuencia**   frequently

¿— **qué frecuencia?**   How frequently?, How often?

conceder un crédito   to extend credit

concubinato (*m.*)   common-law marriage

condado (*m.*)   county

condena (*f.*)   sentence

condición (*f.*)   condition

condón (*m.*)   condom

conducir   to drive

— **a cincuenta millas por hora**   to drive fifty miles per hour

conductor(a) (*m., f.*)   driver

confesar (e:ie)   to confess

confesión (*f.*)   confession

confidencial   confidential

confirmar   to confirm
confuso(a)   confused
congregación (*f.*)   meeting, assembly
conmigo   with me
conocer   to know, to be acquainted with (*a person, a place*)
conocido(a) (*m., f.*)   acquaintance
consecutivo(a)   consecutive
conseguir (e:i)   to get, to obtain, to manage
consejero(a) (*m., f.*)   counselor
  — familiar (*m., f.*)   family counselor
consejo (*m.*)   advice
consentimiento (*m.*)   consent
conserve su derecha   keep to the right (*traffic sign*)
considerar   to consider
consigo   with him, with her, with you (*formal*)
consistir (en)   to consist (of)
consulado (*m.*)   consulate
consultar   to consult
contacto (*m.*)   contact
contagiar   to infect
contagioso(a)   contagious
contar (o:ue)   to count; to tell
contenido (*m.*)   content
contestación (*f.*)   answer
contestar   to answer
contigo   with you (*informal*)
continuar   to continue
contra   against
contrabandear   to smuggle
contrabando (*m.*)   contraband; smuggling
contrato (*m.*)   contract
contribuyente (*m., f.*)   taxpayer

control (*m.*)   control
convaleciente (*m., f.*)   convalescent
convencer   to convince
conveniencia (*f.*)   convenience
conversación (*f.*)   conversation
   — **breve** (*f.*)   brief conversation
conversar   to talk
convertirse (e:ie) en   to change into, to become
cooperación (*f.*)   cooperation
cooperar   to cooperate
copia (*f.*)   copy
   — **fotostática** (*f.*)   photocopy
corazón (*m.*)   heart
corbata (*f.*)   tie
cordón (del zapato) (*m.*)   shoelace
correa (*f.*)   belt
correcto(a)   correct
correo (*m.*)   mail
correr   to run
correspondencia (*f.*)   mail
cortada (*f.*)   cut (*Méx. y Cuba*)
cortadura (*f.*)   cut
cortar (el césped)   to mow, to cut (the lawn)
cortavidrios (*m.*)   glass cutter
corte (*f.*)   court (of law)
cortesía (*f.*)   courtesy
corto(a)   short (*in length*)
cosa (*f.*)   affair, thing
cosméticos (*m. pl.*)   cosmetics
costar (o:ue)   to cost
costo (*m.*)   cost
crac (*m.*)   crack cocaine
creer   to think, to believe
   — **que no**   to not think so

— **que sí**   to think so

crema (*f.*)   cream

crespo(a)   curly

crianza (*f.*)   raising, upbringing

criarse   to be raised

crimen (*m.*)   crime

criminal   criminal

crisis (*f.*)   crisis

cruce (*m.*)   crossing, intersection

— **de niños** (*m.*)   school crossing

crup (*m.*)   croup

cruz (*f.*)   cross; X

— **Roja** (*f.*)   Red Cross

cruzar   to cross

cuadra (*f.*)   block

cuadrado (*m.*)   box; square

cuadro (*m.*)   box; square

¿cuál?   which?, what?

cualquier(a)   any, any (one), either

— **cosa que diga**   anything you say

cuando   when

¿cuándo?   when?

cuanto antes   as soon as possible

¿cuánto(a)?   how much?

   ¿Cuánto paga de alquiler?   How much do
      you pay in rent?

   ¿cuánto tiempo?   how long?

   ¿Cuánto tiempo hace que... ?   How long
      have . . . ?

   ¿Cuánto tiempo hacía que... ?   How long
      had . . . ?

¿cuántos (as)?   how many?

   ¿Cuántos años tiene Ud.?   How old are
      you?

cuarto (*m.*) bedroom, room; quarter
— **de hora** (*m.*) a quarter of an hour
cuarto(a) fourth
cubierta (*f.*) hood
cubierto(a) covered
cubiertos (*m. pl.*) silverware
cubrir to cover
cucaracha (*f.*) cockroach; joint (*coll.*)
cuchillo (*m.*) knife
cuello (*m.*) neck, collar
cuenta (*f.*) bill, account
— **corriente** (*f.*) checking account
— **de ahorros** (*f.*) savings account
— **de cheques** (*f.*) checking account
cuerpo (*m.*) body
cuestionario (*m.*) questionnaire
¡Cuidado! Careful!
cuidado (*m.*) care
cuidar to take care of
culpa (*f.*) blame
culpable guilty
cultural cultural
cuna (*f.*) crib
cuñado(a) (*m., f.*) brother-in-law, sister-in-law
cupón (*m.*) coupon
— **para comida** (*m.*) food stamp
cura (*m.*) (Catholic) priest
curandero(a) (*m., f.*) natural healer
curita (*f.*) band-aid
curso (*m.*) course, class
curva peligrosa (*f.*) dangerous curve (*traffic sign*)
custodia (*f.*) custody
cuyo(a) whose

D

daga (*f.*)   dagger
dar   to give
— **a luz**   to give birth
— **de alta**   to discharge (*from the hospital*)
— **de comer**   to feed, to nurse
— **el pecho**   to nurse
— **fuego**   to set on fire
— **golpe**   to hit, to strike
— **respiración artificial**   to give CPR
— **un tiro (un balazo)**   to shoot
— **un paso**   to take a step
— **una puñalada**   to stab
darle vergüenza a uno   to be embarrassed
darse   to give oneself
— **cuenta de**   to realize, to become aware of
— **preso(a)**   to be under arrest
— **vuelta**   to turn around
dato personal (*m.*)   personal data (information)
datos (*m. pl.*)   information, data
de   of, from, about
— **acuerdo con**   according to
— **al lado**   next-door (*neighbor, house*)
— **cuadros**   plaid
— **cultivo**   cultured (*pearl*)
— **estatura mediana**   of medium height
— **este modo**   in this way
— **(la) mano**   by (the) hand
— **la mañana (tarde, noche)**   in the morning
   (afternoon, evening)
— **lado**   on (one's) side
— **lunares**   polka dot
— **madrugada**   at dawn; at daybreak

— **mangas cortas (largas)** short- (long-) sleeved

— **modo que** so that

— **nada.** You're welcome., Don't mention it.

— **nuevo** over, again

— **ojos (azules)** with (blue) eyes

— **pelo (negro)** with (black) hair

— **primera calidad** first class, top quality

— **rayas** striped

— **rutina** routinely

— **todos modos** anyway

— **vacaciones** on vacation

¿— **veras?** Really?

debajo de under, underneath, below

deber must, should; to owe

— **(+ _inf._)** should (do something), must (do something)

decidir to decide

décimo(a) tenth

decir (e:i) to say, to tell

declaración falsa (_f._) false statement

declarar culpable to convict

dedo (_m._) finger

— **(del) corazón** (_m._) middle finger

— **del pie** (_m._) toe

— **mayor** (_m._) middle finger

deducciones permitidas (_f. pl._) allowable deductions

deducible deductible

defecto físico (_m._) disability

defender(se) to defend (oneself)

defensa propia (_f._) self-defense

deformado(a) deformed

deformar to deform

dejar to leave (behind); to allow, to let
— **de (+ *inf.*)** to fail (to do something); to stop (doing something)
— **encendido(a), prendido(a)** to leave turned on
del (de + el) of the, to the
deletrear to spell
delgado(a) thin
delincuente juvenil (*m., f.*) juvenile delinquent
delírium tremens (*m.*) DT's
delito (*m.*) crime, transgression of law; misdemeanor; felony
— **mayor (grave)** (*m.*) felony
demanda (*f.*) lawsuit
demandar to sue
demás: los (las) — (*m., f.*) (the) others
demasiado(a) excessive, too much
demorar to take (time)
denegado(a) denied
dentadura postiza (*f.*) denture
dental dental
dentro inside
— **de** in, within
denuncia (*f.*) report (of a crime), accusation
denunciar to report (a crime), to accuse
departamento (*m.*) department
— **de Bienestar Social** (*m.*) Social Welfare Department
— **de Protección de Niños** (*m.*) Children's Protection Department
— **de Sanidad** (*m.*) Health Department
depender to depend
dependiente (*m., f.*) dependent; clerk
depósito de seguridad (*m.*) security deposit

depresión nerviosa (*f.*)   nervous depression
derecha (*f.*)   right (direction)
derecho (*m.*)   right (law); (*adv.*) straight ahead
   — **a visitar** (*m.*)   visitation rights
derecho(a)   right
derrame cerebral (*m.*)   stroke
desalojado(a)   homeless
desalojar   to vacate
desalojo (*m.*)   eviction
desaparecer   to disappear
desaparecido(a)   missing
descansar   to rest
descanso (*m.*)   rest, vacation
   — **de primavera** (*m.*)   spring break
descomponerse   to break
descompuesto(a)   broken (down), not working,
  out of order
desconocido(a) (*m., f.*)   stranger
descontar (o:ue)   to deduct
describir   to describe
descripción (*f.*)   description
descuidar   to neglect
desde   from, since
   — **luego**   of course
¡Dése preso(a)!   You're under arrest!
¡Dése vuelta!   Turn around!
desear   to wish, to want
desfigurado(a)   disfigured
desgraciadamente   unfortunately
desintoxicación (*f.*)   detoxification
desocupado(a)   jobless; vacant, empty
desocupar   to vacate
despacio   slowly, slow
despedida (*f.*)   farewell

despedir (e:i)   to fire (*from a job*)
desperfecto (*m.*)   (slight) damage, imperfection
despertar(se) (e:ie)   to wake (someone) up
después (de)   after, afterward; later
desquitar(se)   to get even with
destruir   to destroy
desviarse   to swerve
desvío (*m.*)   detour
detalle (*m.*)   detail
detective (*m., f.*)   detective
detención (*f.*)   detention
detener   to stop, to arrest, to detain
detenido(a)   arrested; (*m., f.*) person under
   arrest
detergente (*m.*)   detergent
determinar   to determine
detrás de la espalda   behind your back
deuda (*f.*)   debt
día (*m.*)   day
   — **de fiesta** (*m.*)   holiday
   — **feriado** (*m.*)   holiday
diabetes (*f.*)   diabetes
diagnóstico (*m.*)   diagnosis
diario (*m.*)   newspaper
diario(a)   daily; per day
diarrea (*f.*)   diarrhea
dictar sentencia   to sentence
diente (*m.*)   tooth
diferente   different
difícil   difficult
dificultad (*f.*)   difficulty
   — **del habla** (*f.*)   speech impediment
Diga.   Hello. (*on the telephone*) (*Cuba y España*)
dinamita (*f.*)   dynamite

dinero (*m.*) money
Dios quiera I hope (God grant)
diploma (*m.*) diploma
dirección (*f.*) address
directamente directly
director(a) (*m., f.*) **(de la escuela)** principal (at a school)
directorio telefónico (*m.*) telephone book
disciplina (*f.*) discipline
disciplinar to discipline
disco compacto (*m.*) compact disc
discriminación (*f.*) discrimination
discutir to discuss
disgustado(a) upset
disparar to shoot
dispersarse to disperse
disponible available
dispuesto(a) willing
distribuir to distribute
distrito (*m.*) area
dividendo (*m.*) dividend
división (*f.*) section, division
divorciado(a) divorced
divorciarse to divorce
doblar to turn
doble double
   — circulación (*f.*) two-way traffic
   — vía (*f.*) divided road
doctor(a) (*m., f.*) doctor
documento (*m.*) document
   — falso (*m.*) forged document
dólar (*m.*) dollar
doler (o:ue) to hurt, to ache
dolor (*m.*) pain, ache

domicilio (*m.*)   address, domicile
¿dónde?   where?
dormido(a)   asleep
dormir (o:ue)   to sleep
dormitorio (*m.*)   bedroom
dorso (*m.*)   back (*of paper*)
dos veces   twice
droga (*f.*)   drug
drogadicto(a) (*m., f.*)   drug addict
droguero(a) (*m., f.*)   drug user, drug pusher
ducharse   to shower
dudar   to doubt
dueño(a) (*m., f.*)   owner
   — de la casa (*m., f.*)   landlord, landlady
durante   during
   — el día (la noche)   during the day (night)
durar   to last
duro(a)   hard; difficult

E

echar   to throw
   — la cabeza hacia atrás   to tilt one's head
      back
económico(a)   financial
edad (*f.*)   age
edificio (*m.*)   building
el (la) que   the one who
electricidad (*f.*)   electricity
electrodoméstico (*m.*)   electrical (household)
   appliance
elegibilidad (*f.*)   eligibility
elegible   eligible
elegido(a)   chosen

elegir (e:i)   to choose
embarazada   pregnant
embarazo (*m.*)   pregnancy
embolia (*f.*)   blood clot, stroke
emborracharse   to get drunk
embrague (*m.*)   gearshift lever; clutch
emergencia (*f.*)   emergency
empeñar   to pawn
empezar (e:ie)   to begin
empleado(a) (*m., f.*)   employee, clerk
empleador (*m.*)   employer
empleo (*m.*)   job
empujar   to push
en   at, in
  — **bicicleta**   on a bike
  — **buena parte**   to a large extent
  — **casa**   at home
  — **caso de**   in case of
  — **contra de**   against
  — **cuanto**   as soon as
  — **defensa propia**   in self-defense
  — **efectivo**   in cash
  — **ese caso**   in that case
  — **estas situaciones**   in these situations
  — **este momento**   at the moment
  — **libertad bajo fianza**   out on bail
  — **libertad bajo palabra**   out on one's own
     recognizance
  — **libertad condicional**   out on probation
  — **lugar de**   instead of
  — **persona**   personally, in person
  — **primer lugar**   in the first place
  ¿— **qué puedo ayudarle?**   What can I do for
     you?

¿**— qué puedo servirle?** How may I help you?

— **seguida** right away

— **sentido contrario** in the opposite direction

— **uso** in use

encargarse (de) to be in charge (of)

encender (e:ie) to turn on (*a light*)

encendido(a) on, turned on (*a light, a TV set*)

encerrado(a) locked up, closeted

encerrar (e:ie) to lock up

enchufe (*m.*) electrical outlet, socket

encontrar (o:ue) to find

endrogado(a) on drugs

endrogarse to take drugs; to become addicted to drugs

enfermarse to get sick, to fall ill

enfermedad (*f.*) disease, sickness

— **venérea** (*f.*) venereal disease

enfermero(a) (*m., f.*) nurse

— **visitador(a)** (*m., f.*) visiting nurse

enfermo(a) sick, ill

enfrente de across the street from

enganche (*m.*) down payment (*Méx.*)

engañar to cheat, to deceive

enojado(a) angry

enseguida right away

enseñar to show

entender (e:ie) to understand

enterarse de to find out about

entonces then

entrada (*f.*) income; entrance; down payment

— **bruta** (*f.*) gross earnings

— **neta** (*f.*) net income

entrar (en) to go in, to enter
  no entre do not enter; wrong way (*traffic signs*)
entre between, among
entrega (*f.*) delivery
entregar to give, to turn over (something to someone)
entrelazar to interlace, to intertwine
entremeterse to meddle, to butt in
entrenado(a) trained
entrenamiento (*m.*) training
entrevista (*f.*) interview
entrevistar to interview
entrometerse to meddle, to butt in
envenenar(se) to poison (oneself)
enviar to send
epidemia (*f.*) epidemic
epiléptico(a) epileptic
equipo (*m.*) equipment
  — **electrodoméstico** (*m.*) electrical (household) appliance
equis (*f.*) cross
es it is
  — **cierto.** That's right., It's true.
  — **de unos...** It's about . . .
  — **decir...** That is to say . . .
  — **que...** It's just that . . .
escala de soga (*f.*) rope ladder
escalera (*f.*) stairs
  — **de mano** (*f.*) hand ladder
escaparse to run away
escoger to choose
escopeta (*f.*) shotgun

escribir   to write
   — a máquina   to type
escritorio (*m.*)   desk
escuela (*f.*)   school; school crossing
   — primaria (elemental) (*f.*)   grade school
   — nocturna (*f.*)   night school
   — secundaria (*f.*)   secondary school (junior
      and high school)
escusado (*m.*)   bathroom (*Méx.*)
ese(a)   that
ése(a) (*m., f.*)   that one
esencial   essential
eso   that
   — es todo.   That's all.
espacio en blanco (*m.*)   blank space
espalda (*f.*)   back
español (*m.*)   Spanish (language)
esparadrapo (*m.*)   adhesive tape
especial   special
especialista (*m., f.*)   specialist
especificar   to specify
espejo (*m.*)   mirror
espejuelos (*m. pl.*)   eyeglasses (*Cuba y Puerto
   Rico*)
esperar   to wait (for); to hope
esposado(a)   handcuffed
esposas (*f. pl.*)   handcuffs
esposo(a) (*m., f.*)   husband, wife
esquina (*f.*)   corner
ésta   this one
esta (*f.*)   this
   — noche   tonight
   — vez   this time
Está bien.   Okay., That's fine.

establecer to establish
estación (*f.*) station
  — **de bomberos** (*f.*) fire department
  — **de correos** (*f.*) post office
  — **de ómnibus (autobuses)** (*f.*) bus station
  — **de policía** (*f.*) police station
  — **de servicio** (*f.*) gas station
estacionado(a) parked
estacionamiento de emergencia
  solamente emergency parking only
estado (*m.*) state, status
  — **civil** (*m.*) marital status
estafa (*f.*) swindle, fraud
estafar to swindle
estampado(a) print
estampilla para alimento (*f.*) food stamp
estante (*m.*) bookcase
estar to be
  — **a la vista** to be visible
  — **apurado(a)** to be in a hurry
  — **bien** to be okay
  — **de acuerdo** to agree
  — **de regreso** to be back
  — **de vuelta** to be back
  — **en condiciones de (+ *inf.*)** to be in a
    condition to (do something)
  — **en libertad bajo fianza** to be free on bail
  — **en libertad condicional** to be on
    probation
  — **equivocado(a)** to be wrong
  — **preso(a)** to be in jail, to be under arrest
  — **seguro(a)** to be certain
  — **sin trabajo** to be unemployed (out of
    work)

estatal (*adj.*)   state
estatua (*f.*)   statue
estatura (*f.*)   height
  de — mediana   medium height
este (*m.*)   east
este(a)   this
éste(a) (*m., f.*)   this one
estimado (*m.*)   estimate
estómago (*m.*)   stomach
estos(as)   these
estuche de primeros auxilios (*m.*)   first-aid kit
estudiante (*m., f.*)   student
estudiar   to study
estufa (*f.*)   heater
evidencia (*f.*)   evidence
evitar   to avoid
exactamente   exactly
examen (*m.*)   examination
  — de la vista (*m.*)   eye examination
  — del oído (*m.*)   hearing test
examinar   to examine
excusa (*f.*)   excuse
excusado (*m.*)   bathroom (*Méx.*)
exento(a)   exempt
exigir   to demand
explicar   to explain
explosivo (*m.*)   explosive
expresión (*f.*)   expression
extender (e:ie)   to stretch out, to spread
extinguidor de incendios (*m.*)   fire extinguisher
extintor de incendios (*m.*)   fire extinguisher (*España*)
extra   extra

extranjero(a) (*m., f.*) foreigner; (*adj.*) foreign
extraño(a) strange, unknown; (*m., f.*) stranger

F

fábrica (*f.*) factory
fácilmente easily
factoría (*f.*) factory
falda (*f.*) skirt
fallecido(a) deceased
fallecer to die, to pass away
fallo (*m.*) decision; verdict
falsificación (*f.*) falsification; counterfeit;
    forgery
falsificar to falsify; to counterfeit; to forge
falso(a) forged; fake
faltar to be missing
    — a clase to miss class
familia (*f.*) family
fango (*m.*) mud
farmacia (*f.*) pharmacy, drugstore
faro (*m.*) headlight
fe de bautismo (*f.*) baptism certificate
fecha (*f.*) date
    — de hoy (*f.*) today's date
federal federal
felpudo (*m.*) mat
ferrocarril (*m.*) railroad
fiancista (*m., f.*) bailor, bail bondsman
fianza (*f.*) bail
fichar to book; to log in
fiebre (*f.*) fever
fiesta (*f.*) party
fijo(a) fixed

filtro (*m.*) filter
fin de semana (*m.*) weekend
final (*m.*) end
finanzas (*f. pl.*) finance
firma (*f.*) signature
firmar to sign
fiscal (*m., f.*) prosecutor, district attorney
flaco(a) thin; skinny
flecha, flechita (*f.*) arrow
floreado(a) flowered
foco (*m.*) light
fogón (*m.*) stove
folleto (*m.*) brochure
fondo (*m.*) back
   en el — in the back
fondo mutuo (*m.*) mutual fund
forma (*f.*) form; way
fórmula (*f.*) formula
forzar (o:ue) to force
fósforo (*m.*) match
fotocopia (*f.*) photocopy
fotografía (*f.*) photograph
fractura (*f.*) fracture
frecuencia: ¿Con qué —? How frequently?
frecuentemente frequently
freno (*m.*) brake
frente (*f.*) forehead
   — a in front of
frustrado(a) frustrated
fuego (*m.*) fire
   — intencional (*m.*) arson
fuente de ingreso (*f.*) source of income
fuera outside
fugarse to run away

fumar to smoke
futuro (*m.*) future

G

gafas (*f. pl.*) eyeglasses
galleta (*f.*) slap (*Cuba y Puerto Rico*)
ganancia (*f.*) gain; earning, profit
ganar to earn; to gain
ganga (*f.*) bargain
ganzúa (*f.*) skeleton key; picklock
garaje (*m.*) garage
garganta (*f.*) throat
garrotillo (*m.*) croup
gas (*m.*) gas
gasa (*f.*) gauze
gasolina (*f.*) gasoline
gasolinera (*f.*) gas station
gastar to spend (*money*)
gasto (*m.*) expense
— **de la casa** (*m.*) household expense
— **de transportación** (*m.*) transportation
expense
— **funerario** (*m.*) funeral expense
gata (*f.*) jack (*Costa Rica y España*)
gatear to crawl
gato (*m.*) jack
generalmente generally
gente (*f.*) people
golpear to hit, to strike
goma (*f.*) tire
— **ponchada** (*f.*) flat tire
gonorrea (*f.*) gonorrhea
gordo(a) fat

gorra (*f.*)   cap
gorro (*m.*)   hat
grabadora (*f.*)   tape recorder
gracias   thank you
   Muchas —.   Thank you very much.
grado (*m.*)   grade; degree
grafiti (*m.*)   graffiti
gran   great
granada de mano (*f.*)   hand grenade
grande   big, large
grano (*m.*)   pimple
gratis (*adv.*)   free (of charge), without cost
gratuito(a) (*adj.*)   free (of charge)
grave   serious
grifa (*f.*)   hashish (*coll.*)
gripe (*f.*)   flu
gris   gray
gritar   to scream, to shout
grueso(a)   portly
grupo (*m.*)   group
guagua (*f.*)   bus (*Cuba y Puerto Rico*)
guante (*m.*)   glove
guantera (*f.*)   glove compartment
guardado(a)   put away, saved
guardafangos (*m.*)   fender
guardar   to keep, to save
guardería (*f.*)   nursery school
güero(a)   blonde (*Méx.*)
guía de teléfonos (*f.*)   telephone book
guía telefónica (*f.*)   telephone book
gustar   to be pleasing to, to like

H

haber   to have
— **trabajado**   to have worked
había   there was, there were
habitación (*f.*)   bedroom, room
hablar   to speak, to talk
— **con (la) zeta**   to lisp
hace: — **un mes**   a month ago
— **una semana**   a week ago
hacer   to do, to make
— **arreglar**   to have (something) fixed
— **buen tiempo**   to have good weather
— **(mucho) calor**   to be (very) hot
— **caso (a)**   to pay attention (to)
— **falta**   to need
— **(mucho) frío**   to be (very) cold
— **la comida**   to cook (prepare) dinner
— **resistencia**   to resist
— **saber**   to advise, to warn; to let (someone)
   know
— **(mucho) sol**   to be (very) sunny
— **una declaración falsa**   to make a false
   statement
— **una pregunta**   to ask a question
— **(mucho) viento**   to be (very) windy
hacerse   to become
hachich, hachís (*m.*)   hashish
hacia   toward
— **abajo**   down, downward
hasta   until
— **hace poco**   until recently
— **la ...**   up to . . .
— **luego.**   See you later.

— **mañana.** See you tomorrow.

— **que** until

hay there is (there are)

— **de todo.** You can find everything.

No — de qué. You're welcome. Don't mention it.

helado(a) ice, iced

helicóptero (*m.*) helicopter

hepatitis (*f.*) hepatitis

herencia (*f.*) inheritance

herida (*f.*) wound

herido(a) hurt, injured; (*m., f.*) injured person

hermanastro(a) (*m., f.*) stepbrother, stepsister

hermano(a) (*m., f.*) brother; sister

heroína (*f.*) heroin

herpe(s) (*m.*) herpes

hielo (*m.*) ice

hígado (*m.*) liver

hijastro(a) (*m., f.*) stepson; stepdaughter

hijo(a) (*m., f.*) son, daughter

— **de crianza** (*m., f.*) foster child

hijos (*m. pl.*) children, sons

hinchazón (*f.*) bump, swelling

hipertensión (*f.*) hypertension, high blood pressure

hipoteca (*f.*) mortgage

hispánico(a) Hispanic

histéricamente hysterically

historia (*f.*) history

— **clínica** (*f.*) medical history

hogar (*m.*) home

— **de crianza** (*m.*) foster home

— **sustituto** (*m.*) foster home

hoja (*f.*) sheet (of paper)

hola   hello, hi
hombre (*m.*)   man
   — de negocios (*m.*)   businessman
hombro (*m.*)   shoulder
homicidio (*m.*)   manslaughter, homicide
honorario de corredor (*m.*)   broker's fee
hora (*f.*)   time, hour
horario (*m.*)   schedule
horno (*m.*)   oven
hospedaje (*m.*)   lodging
hospital (*m.*)   hospital
hospitalización (*f.*)   hospitalization
hospitalizado(a)   hospitalized
hotel (*m.*)   hotel
hoy   today
   — mismo   this very day
hubo   there was, there were
huelga (*f.*)   strike
huella (*f.*)   footprint
   — digital (*f.*)   fingerprint
humillar   to humiliate
humo (*m.*)   smoke

I

idea (*f.*)   idea
identificación (*f.*)   identification, ID
   — falsa (*f.*)   fake identification, forged ID
identificar   to identify
idioma (*m.*)   language
iglesia (*f.*)   church
ilegal   illegal
impermeable (*m.*)   raincoat

imponer una multa   to impose a fine, to give a ticket

importante   important

importar   to matter

A nadie le importa.   It's nobody's business.

No importa.   It doesn't matter.

imposible   impossible

imprudentemente   imprudently, recklessly

impuesto (*m.*)   tax

— **sobre la propiedad** (*m.*)   property tax

— **sobre la renta** (*m.*)   income tax

incapacidad (*f.*)   disability

incapacitado(a)   incapacitated, handicapped

— **para trabajar**   unable to work

incendiar   to set on fire

incendio (*m.*)   fire

— **intencional** (*m.*)   arson

incesto (*m.*)   incest

incluido(a)   including

incluir   to include

incómodo(a)   uncomfortable

independiente   independent

indicador (*m.*)   turn signal

índice (*m.*)   index finger

infectar   to infect

infiltrar(se)   to infiltrate

influenza (*f.*)   flu

información (*f.*)   information

— **sobre el caso** (*f.*)   case history

informar   to inform, to notify

informe (*m.*)   report

infracción de tránsito (*f.*)   traffic violation

inglés (*m.*)   English (language)

ingresado(a)   admitted (to)

ingresar to be admitted (to), to enter
ingreso (*m.*) income, earnings, revenue
   de bajos ingresos low-income
inicial (*f.*) initial
iniciar to begin, to start, to initiate
inmediatamente immediately
inmigración (*f.*) immigration
inmigrante (*m., f.*) immigrant
   — **ilegal, indocumentado(a)** (*m., f.*) illegal
    immigrant
inocente innocent
inscripción (*f.*) certificate
   — **de bautismo** (*f.*) baptism certificate
   — **de defunción** (*f.*) death certificate
   — **de matrimonio** (*f.*) marriage certificate
   — **de nacimiento** (*f.*) birth certificate (*Cuba*)
insecticida (*m.*) insecticide
instalar to install
intensivo(a) intensive
intérprete (*m., f.*) interpreter
interés (*m.*) interest
interrogar to question, to interrogate
interrogatorio (*m.*) interrogation, questioning
inválido(a) disabled; crippled
inversión (*f.*) investment
investigación (*f.*) investigation
investigador(a) (*m., f.*) investigator; (*adj.*)
   investigating
investigar to investigate
invierno (*m.*) winter
inyección antitetánica (*f.*) tetanus shot
ipecacuana (*f.*) (syrup of) ipecac
ir to go
   — **a (+ *inf.*)** to be going to (do something)

— **y venir**   to commute
irritación (*f.*)   irritation
irse   to go away, to leave
izquierda (*f.*)   left
  a la —   to the left
izquierdo(a)   left

J

jabón (*m.*)   soap
jarabe (*m.*)   syrup
jardín (*m.*)   garden
jardinero(a) (*m., f.*)   gardener
jefatura de policía (*f.*)   police station
jefe(a) (*m., f.*)   chief, boss
  — **de familia** (*m., f.*)   head of household
jeringa hipodérmica (*f.*)   hypodermic syringe
jeringuilla (*f.*)   hypodermic syringe
joven   young; (*m., f.*) young man, young woman
jovencito(a) (*m., f.*)   adolescent, teenager
joya (*f.*)   jewel, jewelry
juanita (*f.*)   marijuana (*coll.*)
jubilación (*f.*)   retirement
jubilado(a)   retired
jubilarse   to retire
judío(a)   Jewish
juez(a) (*m., f.*)   judge
jugar (u:ue)   to play (*a game*)
  — **con fuego**   to play with fire
juguetón(ona)   mischievous, restless
juicio (*m.*)   trial
junta (*f.*)   meeting
juntos(as)   together
jurado (*m.*)   jury

juramento (*m.*)   oath
jurar   to take an oath; to swear
justo(a)   fair
juzgado (*m.*)   court (of law), courthouse
juzgar   to judge

K

kif (*m.*)   hashish

L

la que   the one who
labio (*m.*)   lip
laboratorio (*m.*)   laboratory
lacio(a)   straight (*hair*)
lado (*m.*)   side
ladrillo (*m.*)   1-kilo brick of marijuana (*coll.*)
ladrón(ona) (*m., f.*)   thief, burglar
lámpara (*f.*)   lamp
lápiz (*m.*)   pencil
largo(a)   long
lastimado(a)   hurt, injured
lastimarse   to get hurt, to hurt oneself
latino(a)   Latin, Hispanic
leche (*f.*)   milk
leer   to read
legal   legal
lejía (*f.*)   bleach
lejos   far
   — de   far from
lengua (*f.*)   tongue; language
leño (*m.*)   joint (*coll.*)

lentes (*m. pl.*) eyeglasses
 — de contacto (*m. pl.*) contact lenses
lesión (*f.*) injury
lesionado(a) injured
letra de molde (*f.*) print, printing
levantar to lift
levantarse to get up
ley (*f.*) law
libertad (*f.*) freedom
 — bajo fianza (*f.*) release on bail
 — condicional (*f.*) probation
libra (*f.*) pound
librería (*f.*) bookstore
libreta de ahorros (*f.*) savings passbook
libreta de teléfonos (*f.*) address book
libro (*m.*) book
 — de texto (*m.*) textbook
licencia (*f.*) license
 — de conducir (*f.*) driver's license
 — para cuidar niños (*f.*) child care license
 — para manejar (conducir) (*f.*) driver's
   license
licorería (*f.*) liquor store
limitado(a) limited
límite (*m.*) limit
 — de velocidad (*m.*) speed limit
limpiaparabrisas (*m. sing.*) windshield wiper
limpiar to clean
limpieza (*f.*) cleaning
línea (*f.*) line (*on a paper or form*)
 — de ayuda a los padres (*f.*) parents'
   helpline
 — de parada (*f.*) stop line
linterna (*f.*) flashlight

líquido (*m.*)   liquid
lista (*f.*)   list
listo(a)   ready
llamada (*f.*)   call
 — **telefónica** (*f.*)   phone call
llamar   to call
 — **al perro**   to call off the dog
 — **por teléfono**   to phone
llamarse   to be named, to be called
llanta (*f.*)   tire
 — **pinchada** (*f.*)   flat tire
llave (*f.*)   key
 — **falsa** (*f.*)   skeleton key; picklock
llegar (a)   to arrive (at), to reach
 — **a (+ *inf.*)**   to succeed in (doing something)
 — **tarde**   to be late
llenar   to fill out
llevar   to take (someone or something somewhere), to carry; to wear
 — **puesto(a)**   to wear
llevarse   to steal
 — **bien**   to get along well
llorar   to cry
llover (o:ue)   to rain
lluvia (*f.*)   rain
lo   it; you, him
 — **demás**   the rest
 — **más pronto posible**   as soon as possible
 — **mejor**   the best (thing)
 — **primero**   the first (thing)
 — **que**   what
 — **sé.**   I know.
 — **siento.**   I'm sorry.
 — **suficiente**   enough

local local
loción para bebé (*f.*) baby lotion
los (las) demás (*m., f.*) the others
luchar to fight, to struggle
luego later, afterwards, then
lugar (*m.*) place
  — **de nacimiento** (*m.*) place of birth
lunar (*m.*) mole
  de lunares polka dot
luz (*f.*) light

M

maceta de flores (*f.*) flower pot
machismo (*m.*) male chauvinism
madrastra (*f.*) stepmother
madre (*f.*) mother, mom
madrina (*f.*) godmother
madrugada (*f.*) early morning
madurar to mature
maestro(a) (*m., f.*) teacher
majadero(a) mischievous, restless
mal badly
maletero (*m.*) trunk (*of a car*)
malo(a) bad
maltratar to abuse, to mistreat
maltrato (*m.*) abuse
mamá (*f.*) mother, mom
mamadera (*f.*) baby bottle
mamila (*f.*) baby bottle (*Méx.*)
mancha (*f.*) spot, mark, blemish
manco(a) one-handed
mandar to send
manejar to drive

    — estando borracho(a)   drunk driving
    ¡Maneje con cuidado!   Drive safely!
manera (*f.*)   way, manner
mangas (*f. pl.*)   sleeves
    de — cortas   short-sleeved
    de — largas   long-sleeved
    sin —   sleeveless
Mande.   Hello. (*on the telephone*) (*Méx.*)
manera (*f.*)   way, manner
mano (*f.*)   hand
    ¡Manos arriba!   Hands up!
manteca (*f.*)   heroin (*coll.*) (*Caribe*)
mantener(se) (e:ie)   to keep; to support (oneself)
    mantenga su derecha   keep right (*traffic sign*)
mantequilla (*f.*)   butter
manzana (*f.*)   city block
mañana (*f.*)   morning; (*adv.*) tomorrow
máquina (*f.*)   car (*Cuba*)
maravilloso(a)   wonderful, marvelous
marca (*f.*)   mark; brand, make (*car*)
marcar   to mark, to check off
mareado(a)   dizzy
marido (*m.*)   husband
mariguana, marihuana, marijuana
    (*f.*)   marijuana
más   more
    — bien   rather
    — o menos   more or less
    — ... que (de)   more . . . than
    — que nunca   more than ever
    — tarde   later
máscara (*f.*)   mask
matar   to kill

matrícula (*f.*)   registration
matricularse   to register; to enroll (in a school)
matrimonio (*m.*)   marriage
mayor   older, oldest
  — de edad   of age; adult
  el (la) —   the oldest
mayoría (*f.*)   majority
mecánico (*m.*)   mechanic
media hora (*f.*)   half an hour
mediano(a)   medium; average
medianoche (*f.*)   midnight
  a (la) —   at midnight
medias (*f. pl.*)   stockings
  — de hombre (*f. pl.*)   socks
medicina (*f.*)   medicine
médico(a) (*m., f.*)   doctor; (*adj.*) medical
medio (*adv.*)   rather
medio(a)   half
  — hermano(a) (*m., f.*)   half-brother, half-
    sister
mediodía (*m.*)   midday, noon
medir (e:i)   to measure; to be (*amount*) tall
mejilla (*f.*)   cheek
mejor   better; best
  — que nunca   better than ever
mejorar(se)   to improve, to get better
meñique (*m.*)   little finger
menor   younger, youngest
  el (la) —   the youngest
  — de edad (*m., f.*)   minor
menos (de, que)   less (than), fewer (than)
  — mal   thank goodness
  — ... que   less . . . than
mensaje (*m.*)   message

mensual monthly
mentir (e:ie) to lie, to tell a lie
mentira (f.) lie
mercado (m.) market, supermarket
  — **al aire libre** (m.) open-air market
mes (m.) month
  el — pasado last month
  el — próximo next month
  el — que viene next month
mesa (f.) table
mesita de noche (f.) night table
mestizo(a) mixed race (*any of two or more races*)
metadona (f.) methadone
meterse en la boca to put in one's mouth
metido(a) inside, inserted in
mi(s) my
miembro (m., f.) member
  — **del jurado** (m., f.) jury member
mientras while
  — **tanto** in the meantime
milla (f.) mile
minuto (m.) minute
mirando watching
mirar to look at
Mire. Look.
mismo(a) same
  el (la) — que antes the same as before
  por sí — by himself; by herself
mitin (m.) meeting, assembly
modelo (m.) model
modo (m.) way, manner
molesto(a) annoyed, bothered
momentico (m.) a short time
momentito (m.) a short time

momento (*m.*)   moment
moneda (*f.*)   coin
monumento (*m.*)   monument
morado (*m.*)   bruise
mordaza (*f.*)   gag
mordida (*f.*)   bite
moretón (*m.*)   bruise
morfina (*f.*)   morphine
morgue (*f.*)   morgue
morir (o:ue)   to die, to pass away
mostrador (*m.*)   counter
mostrar (o:ue)   to show
mota (*f.*)   marijuana (*coll.*)
motel (*m.*)   motel
motivo (*m.*)   motive
motocicleta (*f.*)   motorcycle; motor-driven cycle
motor (*m.*)   engine, motor
  — de arranque (*m.*)   starter
mover(se) (o:ue)   to move
  ¡No se mueva(n)!   Don't move!, Freeze!
muchacho(a) (*m., f.*)   young man, young woman
muchísimo(a)   very much
mucho (*adv.*)   much
muchos(as)   many
  Muchas gracias.   Thank you very much.
  muchas veces   many times
mudanza (*f.*)   moving (*to another lodging*)
mudarse   to move (*to another lodging*)
mudo(a)   mute
muebles (*m. pl.*)   furniture
muela (*f.*)   molar; tooth
mujer (*f.*)   woman; wife
  — de negocios (*f.*)   businesswoman
mulato(a)   mixed race (*black and white*)

multa (*f.*)   ticket, fine
multitud (*f.*)   crowd
municipal   municipal
muñeca (*f.*)   wrist
murmurar   to murmur
musculoso(a)   muscular
muy   very

N

nacer   to be born
nacimiento (*m.*)   birth
nacionalidad (*f.*)   nationality
nada   nothing
   — más que   just
nadie   nobody, (not) anyone
nalga (*f.*)   buttock, rump
nalgada (*f.*)   spanking; slap on the buttocks
nariz (*f.*)   nose
navaja (*f.*)   switchblade, razor
Navidad (*f.*)   Christmas
neblina (*f.*)   fog
necesario(a)   necessary
necesidad (*f.*)   need
necesitar   to need
negarse (e:ie)   to refuse to
   — a hablar   to refuse to speak
negativo(a)   negative
negra (*f.*)   black heroin (*coll.*)
negro(a)   black
neto(a)   net
neumático (*m.*)   tire
neumonía (*f.*)   pneumonia
nevar (e:ie)   to snow

ni neither
- **... ni** neither . . . nor
- **un centavo** not a cent

niebla (*f.*) fog

nieto(a) (*m., f.*) grandson, granddaughter

nieve (*f.*) snow

ningún, ninguno(a) no, not any

niñera (*f.*) nanny

niño(a) (*m., f.*) child

no no
- **andar bien** to not go well
- ¡**dispare!** Don't shoot!
- **entre** do not enter, wrong way (*traffic sign*)
- **es así.** It is not that way.
- **hay de qué.** You're welcome.; Don't mention it.
- **importa.** It doesn't matter.
- **importarle a nadie** to be nobody's business
- **más que** just
- **pasar** do not pass (*traffic sign*)
- **rebasar** do not pass (*traffic sign*) (*Méx.*)
- ¡**salte!** Don't jump!
- ¡**se mueva(n)!** Don't move!; Freeze!
- ¡**tire!** Don't shoot!
- **tire basura.** Don't litter.

noche (*f.*) night, evening

nombrar to appoint

nombre (*m.*) name, noun
- **de pila** (*m.*) first name

noreste (*m.*) northeast

noroeste (*m.*) northwest

norte (*m.*) north

norteamericano(a) (North) American
¿Nos va a llevar presos? Are you going to arrest us?
nosotros(as) us, we
nota (*f.*) note
notar to notice
notario(a) público(a) (*m., f.*) notary (public)
notificar to inform, to give notice, to report
novio(a) (*m., f.*) boyfriend, girlfriend
nuera (*f.*) daughter-in-law
nuestro(a) our
nuevo(a) new, fresh
numerado(a) numbered
número (*m.*) number
   — de serie (*m.*) serial number
   — de teléfono (*m.*) phone number
nunca never
   — antes never before

O

o or
objeto (*m.*) object, item
obligar to obligate, to force
obligatorio(a) compulsory
obrero(a) (*m., f.*) worker; laborer
obscenidad (*f.*) obscenity
observar to observe, to watch
obtener to obtain, to get
ocasión (*f.*) occasion
ocupado(a) busy
ocurrir to occur, to happen
oeste (*m.*) west

oficina (*f.*) office
  — de correos (*f.*) post office
oficio (*m.*) trade
ofrecer to offer
oído (*m.*) (inner) ear
Oigo. Hello. (*on the telephone*) (*Cuba*)
oír to hear
ojalá I hope (God grant)
ojo (*m.*) eye
  — de vidrio (*m.*) glass eye
  de ojos (azules) with (blue) eyes
  ojos saltones (*m. pl.*) bulging eyes; bug eyes
olor (*m.*) smell
  — a smell of
olvidarse (de) to forget
ómnibus (*m.*) bus
opción (*f.*) option
operador(a) (*m., f.*) telephone operator,
  dispatcher
operarse to have surgery
opio (*m.*) opium
oportunidad (*f.*) opportunity
opuesto(a) opposite
orden de detención (*f.*) warrant; order
ordenador (*m.*) computer (*España*)
ordenar to order
oreja (*f.*) (outer) ear
organización (*f.*) organization
organizar to organize
original original
orina (*f.*) urine
oro (*m.*) gold
ortopédico(a) orthopedic
oscuro(a) dark

otoño (*m.*)   autumn, fall (season)
otro(a)   other, another
   otra persona (*f.*)   someone else
   otra vez   again, once again
otros(as) (*m. pl., f. pl.*)   the others

P

paciente (*m., f.*)   patient
   — **externo(a)** (*m., f.*)   outpatient
   — **interno(a)** (*m., f.*)   inpatient
paciencia (*f.*)   patience
padrastro (*m.*)   stepfather
padre (*m.*)   father, dad; (Catholic) priest
padres (*m. pl.*)   parents
   — **de crianza** (*m. pl.*)   foster parents
padrino (*m.*)   godfather
pagado(a)   paid (for)
pagar   to pay (for)
   — **a plazos**   to pay in installments
página (*f.*)   page
pago (*m.*)   payment
   — **inicial** (*m.*)   down payment
país (*m.*)   country (nation)
   — **de origen** (*m.*)   country of origin
palabra (*f.*)   word
palanca (de cambio de velocidades)
   (*f.*)   gearshift lever
pálido(a)   pale
paliza (*f.*)   beating, spanking
pana (*f.*)   corduroy
pandilla (*f.*)   gang
pantalón (*m.*)   pants, trousers
pantalones (*m. pl.*)   pants

pañal (*m.*)   diaper
  — desechable (*m.*)   disposable diaper
pañuelo (*m.*)   handkerchief
  — de papel (*m.*)   tissue
papá (*m.*)   dad, father
papel (*m.*)   paper
papeleta (*f.*)   form
paperas (*f. pl.*)   mumps
par: un — de   a couple of
para   for, to, in order to
  — allá   there, over there
  — hoy mismo   for today
  — mí   for me
  — que   so that
  — que lo represente   to represent you
  ¿— qué?   For what reason?, Why?, What for?
  — servirle.   At your service.
  — ti   for you
  — ver si...   to see if . . .
parada (*f.*)   stop
  — de autobuses (*f.*)   bus stop
  — de guaguas (*f.*)   bus stop (*Cuba y Puerto Rico*)
  — de ómnibus (*f.*)   bus stop
paradero (*m.*)   whereabouts
parado(a)   standing
paralítico(a)   paralyzed, disabled
paramédico(a) (*m., f.*)   paramedic
parar   to stop
  ¡Pare!   Stop!
pararse   to stand up
  ¡Párese!   Stand up!
parecer   to seem

pared (*f.*)   wall
pareja (*f.*)   couple
parentesco (*m.*)   relationship (*in the family*)
pariente (*m., f.*)   relative
   —s políticos (*m. pl.*)   in-laws
parir   to give birth
parpadear   to blink
parque (*m.*)   park
parroquial   parochial
parte (*f.*)   part
participar   to take part, to participate
partida (*f.*)   certificate
   — de bautismo (*f.*)   baptism certificate
   — de defunción (*f.*)   death certificate
   — de... dólares (*f.*)   increment of . . . dollars
   — de matrimonio (*f.*)   marriage certificate
   — de nacimiento (*f.*)   birth certificate
pasado (*m.*)   past
   — mañana   the day after tomorrow
pasado(a)   last
pasajero(a) (*m., f.*)   passenger
pasaporte (*m.*)   passport
pasar   to come in; to happen; to pass (a car); to
   spend (time)
   no —   do not pass (*traffic sign*)
   no pase   wrong way; do not enter (*traffic
   sign*)
   — un buen rato   to have a good time
   —lo bien   to have a good time
pasarse la luz roja   to go through a red light
Pase.   Come in.
pasillo (*m.*)   hallway
paso (*m.*)   step
   — de peatones (*m.*)   pedestrian crossing

un — **más** a step further
pastilla (*f.*) pill; LSD (*coll.*)
pasto (*m.*) marijuana (*coll.*)
pastor(a) (*m., f.*) pastor; person of the clergy
pata de cabra (*f.*) crowbar
patada (*f.*) kick
patio (*m.*) backyard, yard
patrón(ona) (*m., f.*) boss
patrono (*m.*) boss (*Cuba*)
patrulla (*f.*) patrol
patrullero(a) (*adj.*) patrol
peatón (*m., f.*) pedestrian
peca (*f.*) freckle
pecho (*m.*) chest
pediatra (*m., f.*) pediatrician
pedir (e:i) to ask for, to request
  — **ayuda** to apply for aid
  — **un favor** to ask a favor
  — **prestado(a)** to borrow
  Pida ver... Ask to see . . .
pegao (*m.*) LSD (*coll.*)
pegar to beat, to hit, to strike
  — **fuego** to set on fire
  — **un tiro (un balazo)** to shoot
peine (*m.*) comb
pelado(a) bald
pelea (*f.*) fight
peligro (*m.*) danger
peligroso(a) dangerous
pelirrojo(a) red-haired
pelo (*m.*) hair
pelón(ona) bald
pelota (*f.*) ball
peluca (*f.*) wig; hairpiece

pena (*f.*)   penalty
penalidad (*f.*)   penalty
penetración (*f.*)   penetration
pensar (e:ie)   to think
  — (+ *inf.*)   to plan (to do something)
  — **en eso**   to think about that
pensión (*f.*)   pension
  — **alimenticia** (*f.*)   child support, alimony
pensionado(a)   retired
peor   worse
pequeño(a)   small, little
perder (e:ie)   to lose
pérdida (*f.*)   loss
perdido(a)   lost
perdón   pardon me, excuse me
perdón (*m.*)   pardon, forgiveness
perdonar   to pardon, to forgive
perfecto(a)   perfect
perico (*m.*)   cocaine (*coll.*)
periódico (*m.*)   newspaper
perito (*m., f.*)   expert
perjudicar   to cause damage, to hurt
perla (*f.*)   pearl
permanecer   to stay, to remain
permanente   permanent
permiso (*m.*)   permission
  — **de detención** (*m.*)   warrant; order
  — **de trabajo** (*m.*)   work permit
permitido(a)   allowable, permitted
pero   but
persona (*f.*)   person
  — **extraña** (*f.*)   stranger
personal   personal; (*m.*) staff, personnel
pertenencia (*f.*)   belonging

pesar to weigh
peso (*m.*) weight
pestaña (*f.*) eyelash
pico (*m.*) bit, small amount
pie (*m.*) foot
piedra (*f.*) rock (crack cocaine) (*coll.*); stone, rock
piel (*f.*) skin
pierna (*f.*) leg
píldora (*f.*) pill
pinta (*f.*) pint
pintura (*f.*) paint
pinzas (*f. pl.*) tweezers
piscina (*f.*) swimming pool
piso (*m.*) floor
pista (*f.*) clue
pistola (*f.*) pistol
pito (*m.*) marijuana (*coll.*)
placa (*f.*) license plate
plancha (*f.*) iron (*for clothes*)
planilla (*f.*) form
plata (*f.*) silver
playa (*f.*) beach
plazo (*m.*) installment, term
   a —s on installments
pobre poor
poco (*m.*) little (*quantity*)
poco(a) little
pocos(as) few
podar arbustos (árboles) to trim bushes (trees)
poder (o:ue) can, to be able
   No se puede escribir... You (one) cannot write . . .
   puede usarse can be used

policía (*f.*) police (force); (*m.*, *f.*) police officer
  — **secreta** (*f.*) undercover police
policlínica (*f.*) clinic; hospital
póliza (*f.*) policy
polvo (*m.*) cocaine (*coll.*)
poner to make, to put
  — **en peligro** to endanger
  — **las manos en la pared** to put one's hands
    against the wall
  — **violento(a)** to make violent
ponerse to put on
  — **azul** to turn blue
  — **blanco(a)** to turn white
  — **de pie** to stand up
  — **de rodillas** to get on one's knees
  — **en contacto** to get in touch
  — **pálido(a)** to turn pale
  — **rojo(a)** to turn red
por for
  — **ciento** (*m.*) percent
  — **completo** completely
  — **correo** by mail
  — **culpa de** because of
  — **desgracia** unfortunately
  — **día** daily, per day
  — **ejemplo** for example
  — **enfermedad** due to illness
  — **escrito** in writing
  — **eso** that's why, for that reason
  — **favor** please
  — **la mañana** in the morning
  — **la noche** in the evening, at night
  — **la tarde** in the afternoon
  — **lo menos** at least

— **lo tanto**   therefore, so
— **mí**   for me
— **poseer drogas**   for possession of drugs
¿— **qué?**   why?
— **semana**   weekly, per week
— **sí mismo(a)**   by himself, by herself
— **suerte**   luckily, fortunately
— **teléfono**   on the phone, by phone
— **un tiempo**   for a while
pornográfico(a)   pornographic
porque   because
porqué (*m.*)   reason
porro (*m.*)   joint (*coll.*)
portaequipajes (*m.*)   trunk (*of a car*)
portaguantes (*m.*)   glove compartment
portal (*m.*)   porch
portarse   to behave
— **mal**   to misbehave
poseer   to own
posibilidad (*f.*)   possibility
posible   possible
posiblemente   possibly
posición (*f.*)   position
postal   postal
practicar   to practice
precaución (*f.*)   precaution
preferir (e:ie)   to prefer
pregunta (*f.*)   question
preguntar   to ask
preliminar   preliminary
prender   to arrest; to turn on (*a light*)
prendido(a)   (turned) on (*a light, a TV set*), lit
preocupado(a)   worried
preocuparse   to worry

preparar   to prepare
presentar   to introduce, to present, to file
   — una apelación   to file an appeal
   — una demanda   to file a lawsuit
presente (*m., adj.*)   present
preservativo (*m.*)   condom
presión (*f.*)   pressure
   — alta (*f.*)   hypertension, high blood pressure
preso(a)   arrested; (*m., f.*) prisoner
préstamo (*m.*)   loan
prestar   to lend
   — atención (a)   to pay attention (to)
presupuesto (*m.*)   budget
prevenir (e:ie)   to prevent
preventivo(a)   preventive
prima (*f.*)   premium
primavera (*f.*)   spring
primero(a) (*adv.*)   first
primeros auxilios (*m. pl.*)   first aid
primo(a) (*m., f.*)   cousin
principal   main
prisión (*f.*)   prison, jail
privado(a)   private
probable   probable
problema (*m.*)   problem
procesado(a)   indicted
profesión (*f.*)   profession
programa (*m.*)   program
prohibido(a)   forbidden, prohibited
   — estacionar   no parking (*traffic sign*)
   — pasar   no trespassing (*traffic sign*)
prohibir   to forbid, to prohibit
promedio (*m.*)   average
prometer   to promise

prometido(a) (*m., f.*) fiancé(e)
pronto soon
propiedad (*f.*) property, asset
   — privada (*f.*) private property
propio(a) own
proporcionar to provide
prostitución (*f.*) prostitution
prostituto(a) (*m., f.*) prostitute
proteger to protect
protestante Protestant
protestar to complain, to protest
provenir (e:ie) to come from; to originate
provisional provisional
próximo(a) next
proyecto de la ciudad (*m.*) city (housing)
   project
prueba (*f.*) proof, evidence; test
   — del alcohol (*f.*) sobriety test
psicólogo(a) (*m., f.*) psychologist
público(a) public
pueblo (*m.*) town
puede ser... it may be . . .
puerta (*f.*) door
   — de la calle (*f.*) front door
   — de salida (*f.*) exit door
pulgada (*f.*) inch
pulgar (*m.*) thumb
pullar to shoot up (drugs) (*Caribe*)
pulmón (*m.*) lung
pulmonía (*f.*) pneumonia
puñal (*m.*) dagger
puñalada (*f.*) stabbing
   dar una — to stab
puñetazo (*m.*) punch

puño (*m.*) fist
punta (*f.*) end, tip
pus (*m.*) pus

Q

que that
　¡— **le vaya bien!** Good luck!
　¡— **se mejore!** Get well soon!
¿qué? what?, which?
　¡— **bueno!** That's great!
　¿— **edad tiene?** How old are you?
　¿— **hay de nuevo?** What's new?
　¿— **hora era (es)?** What time was (is) it?
　¿— **más?** What else?
　¿— **necesita?** What do you (does he/she)
　　need?
　¿— **pasa?** What's happening?
　¿— **se le ofrece?** What can I (we) do for you?
　¡— **suerte!** How fortunate!, It's a good thing!,
　　What luck!
　¿— **tal?** How is it going?
　¿— **te pasa?** What's the matter with you?
　¿— **tiene?** What's wrong?
quedar to be located
　declarado(a) ilegal to be hereby declared
　　illegal
quedarse to stay
　— **callado(a)** to remain silent
　— **con** to keep
　— **paralítico(a)** to become paralyzed, to
　　become crippled
　— **quieto(a)** to sit (stay) still
　— **sin trabajo** to lose one's job

quehaceres del hogar (de la casa) (*m. pl.*) housework

queja (*f.*) complaint

quejarse to complain

quemadura (*f.*) burn

quemar(se) to burn (oneself)

querer (e:ie) to want, to wish; to love

— **decir** to mean

quiebra (*f.*) bankruptcy

¿quién? whom?, who?

¿quienes? (*pl.*) who?, whom?

quieto(a) still, quiet, calm

¡**Quieto(a)!** Freeze!

químico(a) chemical

quiropráctico(a) (*m., f.*) chiropractor

quitar to take away

quitarse to take off (*clothing*)

quizá(s) perhaps, maybe

R

rabí (*m.*) rabbi

rabino (*m.*) rabbi

radiografía (*f.*) X-ray

rápido quick, quickly, fast

rasguño (*m.*) scratch

rato (*m.*) while

— **libre** (*m.*) free time

ratón (*m.*) mouse

raza (*f.*) race

realizar to do, to perform, to carry out

rebasar to pass (a car) (*Méx.*)

recámara (*f.*) bedroom (*Méx.*)

recepcionista (*m., f.*) receptionist

recertificación (*f.*) recertification
receta (*f.*) prescription
recetado(a) prescribed
recetar to prescribe
recibir to receive
recibo (*m.*) receipt
recién nacido(a) (*m., f.*) newborn baby
reciente recent
recientemente recently
recipiente (*m., f.*) recipient
recitar to recite
reclusorio para menores (*m.*) juvenile hall
recobrar to recover
recoger to pick up
recomendar (e:ie) to recommend
reconciliación (*f.*) reconciliation
reconocer to recognize
recordar (o:ue) to remember
recurrir (a) to turn (to)
reembolso (*m.*) refund
reevaluar to reevaluate
reformatorio (*m.*) reformatory
refrigerador (*m.*) refrigerator
refugiarse to find refuge (shelter)
regalar to give (a gift)
regalo (*m.*) gift, present
registración (*f.*) registration (*Méx.*)
registrado(a) registered
registrar to book; to log in
registro (*m.*) registration
reglamento (*m.*) rule
regresar to return, to come back
rehusar to refuse
relacionado(a) related

relaciones sexuales (*f. pl.*)   sexual relations

reloj (*m.*)   watch

renglón (*m.*)   line (*on a paper or form*)

renta (*f.*)   rent; income

renunciar   to resign; to waive

reo(a) (*m., f.*)   defendant

reorientación vocacional (*f.*)   vocational training

reparación (*f.*)   repair

reporte (*m.*)   report

representar   to represent

requerido(a)   required

resbalar   to slip

rescatar   to rescue, to ransom

rescate (*m.*)   ransom

resfrío (*m.*)   cold

residencia (*f.*)   residence

residencial   residential

residente (*m., f.*)   resident

resistencia a la autoridad (*f.*)   resisting arrest

resolver (o:ue)   to solve

respirar   to breathe

responder   to respond

responsable   responsible

respuesta (*f.*)   answer

restaurante (*m.*)   restaurant

resto (*m.*)   rest

retirado(a)   retired

retirar(se)   to withdraw; to retire

retiro (*m.*)   retirement

retratar   to photograph

reumatismo (*m.*)   rheumatism

reunión (*f.*)   meeting, assembly

reverso (*m.*)   reverse, back (*of a page*)

revisión (*f.*) review
revista (*f.*) magazine
revólver (*m.*) revolver
rico(a) rich
riego (*m.*) watering
riesgo (*m.*) risk
rifle (*m.*) rifle
rincón (*m.*) corner
riña (*f.*) fight
riñón (*m.*) kidney
rizado(a) curly
rizo(a) curly
robado(a) stolen
robar to rob, to steal from
robo (*m.*) robbery, burglary
roca (*f.*) crack cocaine (*coll.*)
rodilla (*f.*) knee
rojo(a) red
romper to break
rondar to prowl
ropa (*f.*) clothes, clothing
rubio(a) blond(e)
rueda (*f.*) wheel
ruido (*m.*) noise

S

saber to know (something)
sacar to take out
sacerdote (*m.*) priest
saco (*m.*) jacket
sala (*f.*) living room
    — de emergencia (*f.*) emergency room
    — de estar (*f.*) family room, den

salario (*m.*)   salary
saldo (*m.*)   balance (*of a bank account*)
salida (*f.*)   exit
salir   to get (go) out, to leave, to come out
   — con   to go out with, to date
saltar   to jump
salud (*f.*)   health
¡Salud!   To your health!
saludar   to greet
saludo (*m.*)   greeting
salvar   to save (*to rescue*)
sandalia (*f.*)   sandal
sangrar   to bleed
sangre (*f.*)   blood
sarampión (*m.*)   measles
sargento (*m.*)   sergeant
sección (*f.*)   section, division
   — Protectora de Niños (*f.*)   Children's
   Protection Department
seco(a)   dry
secreto(a)   secret
secuestrar   to kidnap
secuestro (*m.*)   kidnapping
sedante (*m.*)   sedative, tranquilizer
sedativo (*m.*)   sedative
seguir (e:i)   to continue, to follow
   — caminando   to keep walking
   — derecho   to go straight ahead
según   according to
segundo(a)   second
   segundo nombre (*m.*)   middle name
seguro (*m.*)   insurance
   — de hospitalización (*m.*)   hospital
   insurance

— **de salud** (*m.*)   health insurance
— **de vida** (*m.*)   life insurance
— **ferroviario** (*m.*)   railroad insurance
— **médico** (*m.*)   medical insurance
— **Social** (*m.*)   Social Security
seguro(a)   sure, safe
sellado(a)   sealed
sello (*m.*)   LSD (*coll.*)
semáforo (*m.*)   traffic light
semana (*f.*)   week
  la — entrante   next week
  la — pasada   last week
  la — próxima   next week
  la — que viene   next week
semanalmente   weekly
semestre (*m.*)   semester
semiautomático(a)   semiautomatic
semiprivado(a)   semiprivate
seno (*m.*)   breast
sentarse (e:ie)   to sit down
  Siéntese.   Sit down.
sentenciar   to sentence
sentimental   sentimental
sentir (e:ie) que   to regret that
  Lo siento.   I'm sorry.
sentirse (e:ie)   to feel
señal de tránsito (*f.*)   traffic sign
señor (Sr.) (*m.*)   Mr., sir, gentleman
  los señores (Ruiz) (*m. pl.*)   Mr. and Mrs.
    Ruiz
señora (Sra.) (*f.*)   Mrs., lady, Ma'am, Madam,
  wife
señorita (Srta.) (*f.*)   Miss, young lady
separación (*f.*)   separation

separado(a)   separated
separar los pies   to separate (spread) one's feet
ser   to be
  — cierto   to be true
  — como las (+ *time*)   to be about (+ *time*)
  — culpable (de)   to be at fault, to be guilty
    (of)
serie (*f.*)   series
serio(a)   serious
serrucho de mano (*m.*)   handsaw
servicio (*m.*)   service
  — gratuito (*m.*)   free service
servir (e:i)   to serve
  para servirle   at your service
sexo (*m.*)   sex; gender
sexto(a)   sixth
sexual   sexual
Sgto. (*abbreviation of* **sargento**)   sergeant
shorts (*m. pl.*)   shorts
si   if
  — es posible   if possible
sí   yes
sí mismo(a)   yourself (*form.*), himself, herself
**SIDA (síndrome de inmunodeficiencia
  adquirida)** (*m.*)   AIDS
siempre   always
Siéntese.   Sit down.
sierra de mano (*f.*)   handsaw
sífilis (*f.*)   syphilis
significar   to mean
siguiente   following
  lo —   the following
silenciador (*m.*)   muffler
silla (*f.*)   chair

— de ruedas (*f.*)   wheelchair
sillón (*m.*)   armchair
simplemente   simply
sin   without
   — embargo   nevertheless, however
   — falta   without fail
   — hogar   homeless
   — mangas   sleeveless
sinagoga (*f.*)   synagogue, temple
sinceramente   sincerely
síntoma (*m.*)   symptom
sirviente(a) (*m., f.*)   servant
sistema (*m.*)   system
situación (*f.*)   situation
soborno (*m.*)   bribe
sobre (*prep.*)   about; on, on top of
   — todo   especially, above all
sobre (*m.*)   envelope
sobredosis (*f.*)   overdose
sobrellevar   to bear, to put up with
sobrino(a) (*m., f.*)   nephew; niece
social   social
¡Socorro!   Help!
sofá (*m.*)   sofa
soga (*f.*)   rope
sol (*m.*)   sun
solamente   only
solicitante (*m., f.*)   applicant
solicitar   to apply for, to ask for, to solicit
   Solicite ver...   Ask to see . . .
solicitud (*f.*)   application
solo(a)   alone
sólo (*adv.*)   only

soltar (o:ue) to let go of
— **el arma** to drop the gun (weapon)
soltero(a) single
sombreado(a) shaded
sombrero (*m.*) hat
someterse a to submit (oneself) to
Somos (+ *number*). There are (+ *number*) of us.
Son las (+ *time*). It's (+ *time*).
sonograma (*m.*) sonogram
sordo(a) deaf
sortija (*f.*) ring
sospecha (*f.*) suspicion
sospechar to suspect
sospechoso(a) suspicious
sótano (*m.*) basement
su(s) your (*form.*), his, her, their
subir to get in (*a car, etc.*); to climb, to go up
Súbase al carro. Get in the car.
subsidio (*m.*) subsidy
subvención (*f.*) subsidy
suceder to happen
sucio(a) dirty
suegro(a) (*m., f.*) father-in-law; mother-in-law
sueldo (*m.*) salary
suelo (*m.*) floor
suéter (*m.*) sweater
suficiente sufficient, enough
sugerir (e:ie) to suggest
suicidarse to commit suicide
supermercado (*m.*) supermarket, market
supervisor(a) (*m., f.*) supervisor
superviviente (*m., f.*) survivor
suplementario(a) supplemental
sur (*m.*) south

sureste (*m.*) southeast
suroeste (*m.*) southwest
suscripción (*f.*) subscription
suspender la entrega to stop delivery
— **de la correspondencia** to stop mail delivery
— **del periódico** to stop newspaper delivery
suyo(a) yours (*form.*)

T

tabique (*m.*) 1-kilo brick of marijuana (*coll.*)
tal such
— **cosa** such a thing
— **vez** perhaps
talón (*m.*) heel
talonario de cheques (*m.*) checkbook
tamaño (*m.*) size
también also, too
tampoco either
tan as, so
—**... como** as . . . as
— **pronto como** as soon as
tanto tiempo so long
tantos(as) so many
tapa de seguridad (*f.*) safety cap, safety cover
tapar to cover; to block
tapicería (*f.*) upholstery
tartamudo(a) (*m., f.*) person who stutters
taquígrafo(a) (*m., f.*) court reporter; stenographer
tarde (*f.*) afternoon; (*adv.*) late
tareas de la casa (*f. pl.*) housework

tarjeta (*f.*)   card
   — **de crédito** (*f.*)   credit card
   — **de inmigración** (*f.*)   immigration card
   — **de Seguro Social** (*f.*)   Social Security card
tartamudear   to stutter
tatuaje (*m.*)   tattoo
teatro (*m.*)   (movie) theater
techo (de tejas) (*m.*)   (tile) roof; ceiling
técnico(a) (*m., f.*)   technician
telefónico(a)   telephone; telephonic
telefonista (*m., f.*)   operator; dispatcher
teléfono (*m.*)   telephone
televisor (*m.*)   television set
temblar (e:ie)   to shake, to tremble, to shiver
temer   to be afraid, to fear
temporal   temporary
temprano   early
tener   to have
   — **a su cargo**   to be in charge of
   — **(+ *number*) años**   to be (+ *number*) years
     old
   — **casa propia**   to own a house
   — **cuidado**   to be careful
   — **derecho a**   to have the right to
   — **hambre**   to be hungry
   — **la culpa (de)**   to be at fault; to be guilty
   — **(mucho) miedo**   to be (very) afraid,
     scared
   — **(mucho) sueño**   to be (very) sleepy
   — **prisa**   to be in a hurry
   — **puesto(a)**   to have on, to wear
   — **que (+ *inf.*)**   to have to (do something)
   — **razón**   to be right
   — **suerte**   to be lucky

— **tanto miedo**   to be so scared
teniente   lieutenant
tensión familiar (*f.*)   family tension
tequila (*f.*)   tequila
terapia física (*f.*)   physical therapy
tercero(a)   third
terminar   to finish; to end
— **de (+ *inf.*)**   to finish (doing something)
término (*m.*)   term
termómetro (*m.*)   thermometer
terraza (*f.*)   terrace
terremoto (*m.*)   earthquake
terrible   terrible
testigo (*m., f.*)   witness
tete (*m.*)   pacifier (*Cuba*)
tía (*f.*)   aunt
tianguis (*m.*)   open-air market (*Méx.*)
tiempo (*m.*)   time
— **libre** (*m.*)   free time
tienda (*f.*)   store
tijeras (*f. pl.*)   scissors
timón (*m.*)   steering wheel (*Cuba*)
tina (*f.*)   bathtub (*Méx.*)
tinta (*f.*)   ink
tío (*m.*)   uncle
tipo (*m.*)   type
tirar   to throw away; to shoot
título (*m.*)   title; diploma
toallita (*f.*)   washcloth
tobilleras (*f. pl.*)   socks (*Méx.*)
tobillo (*m.*)   ankle
tocadiscos (*m.*)   record player
tocar   to touch
— **a la puerta**   to knock at the door

— **el timbre** to ring the door bell

— **la bocina** to honk the horn

todavía yet, still

todo (*m.*) whole, all, everything

— **el día** all day long

— **lo posible** everything possible

todo(a) whole, all, every

todos(as) all, every(body)

todos los días every day

tomacorrientes (*m. sing.*) electrical outlet, socket

tomar to drink, to take

— **asiento** to take a seat

— **las huellas digitales** to fingerprint

— **medidas** to take measures

— **un idioma** to take (study) a language

— **una decisión** to make a decision

tontería (*f.*) foolishness, nonsense

toque de queda (*m.*) curfew

tos (*f.*) cough

toser to cough

total (*m.*) total

totalmente totally

trabajador(a) (*m., f.*) worker

— **agrícola** (*m., f.*) farm worker

— **social** (*m., f.*) social worker

trabajar to work

— **medio día** to work part-time

— **parte del tiempo** to work part-time

— **por cuenta propia** to be self-employed

— **por su cuenta** to be self-employed

— **tiempo completo** to work full-time

trabajo (*m.*) work, job

— **de la casa** (*m.*) housework

traductor(a) (*m., f.*)   translator
traer   to bring
tráfico (*m.*)   traffic
— **lento** (*m.*)   slow traffic
trago (*m.*)   drink
traje (*m.*)   suit
trámites de divorcio (*m. pl.*)   divorce
  proceedings
transfusión (*f.*)   transfusion
tránsito (*m.*)   traffic
tratamiento (*m.*)   treatment
tratar (de)   to try (to); to treat
travesura (*f.*)   mischief, prank
travieso(a)   mischievous; restless
tribunal (*m.*)   court; court house
— **de menores** (*m.*)   juvenile court
— **supremo** (*m.*)   Supreme Court
trimestre (*m.*)   quarter (*three months*)
trompada (*f.*)   punch
Tte. (*abbreviation of* teniente)   Lieutenant
tu   your (*informal*)
tuberculosis (*f.*)   tuberculosis
tuerto(a)   one-eyed
tumor (*m.*)   tumor
turno (*m.*)   appointment
tutor(a) (*m., f.*)   guardian

U

últimamente   last, lately
último(a)   last (in a series)
un, una   a, an
ungüento (*m.*)   ointment
único(a)   only

unido(a) united
unos(as) about, around
urgente urgent
urgentemente urgently
usado(a) used
usar to use
  se usará will be used
uso (*m.*) use
usual usual
  no — unusual
útil useful
utilizar to use

V

va a haber there is going to be
vacaciones (*f. pl.*) vacation
  — de primavera (*f. pl.*) spring break
  de — on vacation
vaciar to empty
vacunar to vaccinate, to immunize
vagina (*f.*) vagina
valer to be worth
válido(a) valid
valor (*m.*) value
Vamos. Let's go.
  — a (+ verb) Let's (+ *verb*).
  — a ver. Let's see.
vandalismo (*m.*) vandalism
varicela (*f.*) chickenpox
varios(as) several
vecindario (*m.*) neighborhood
vecino(a) (*m., f.*) neighbor
vehículo (*m.*) vehicle

veinte twenty
vello (*m.*) body hair
velludo(a) hairy
velocidad (*f.*) speed
  — **máxima** (*f.*) speed limit
vencer to expire
venda (*f.*) bandage
vendaje (*m.*) bandage
vender to sell
veneno (*m.*) poison
venéreo(a) venereal
venir (e:ie) to come
ventana (*f.*) window
ventanilla (*f.*) window (*of a car*)
ver to see
verano (*m.*) summer
verbo (*m.*) verb
verdad (*f.*) truth
  ¿—? right?, true?
verdadero(a) true, real
verde green
veredicto (*m.*) verdict
verificación (*f.*) verification
verificar to verify
verruga (*f.*) wart
vestido (*m.*) dress
vestido(a) dressed
veterinario(a) veterinary
vez (*f.*) time
vía (*f.*) lane
viaje (*m.*) trip
víctima (*f.*) victim
vida (*f.*) life
videocámara (*f.*) video camera

videocasetera (*f.*)   videocassette recorder (VCR)
videograbadora (*f.*)   videocassette recorder (VCR)
viejo(a)   old
vigilancia del barrio (*f.*)   neighborhood watch
vino (*m.*)   wine
violación (*f.*)   rape
violar   to rape
violencia doméstica (*f.*)   domestic violence
violento(a)   violent
virarse (*Cuba*)   to turn around
virus de inmunodeficiencia humana (VIH)   HIV
visa de estudiante (*f.*)   student visa
visible   visible
visitador(a) social (*m., f.*)   social worker who makes home visits
visitar   to visit
vista (*f.*)   (court) hearing
visto(a)   seen
viudo(a) (*m., f.*)   widower, widow; (*adj.*) widowed
vivienda (*f.*)   home, lodging
vivir   to live
vocabulario (*m.*)   vocabulary
volante (*m.*)   steering wheel
voltear(se) (*Méx.*)   to turn around
voluntad (*f.*)   will
voluntariamente   voluntarily
volver (o:ue)   to come (go) back, to return

Y

y   and

ya   already; at last, finally
— **están en camino.**   They are (already) on
  their way.
— **no**   no longer
yerba (*f.*)   marijuana (coll.)
yerno (*m.*)   son-in-law
yesca (*f.*)   marijuana (coll.)
yo mismo(a)   myself

Z

zacate (*m.*)   lawn (*Méx.*); marijuana (*coll.*)
zapato (*m.*)   shoe
— **de tenis** (*m.*)   tennis shoe
zona (*f.*)   zone
— **de estacionamiento** (*f.*)   parking lot
— **postal** (*f.*)   zip code, postal code
zurdo(a)   left-handed

English–Spanish

A

a   un, una
— **(per) day**   al día
— **little**   un poco
— **week**   a la semana
— **week ago**   hace una semana
— **while later**   al rato

able   capacitado(a)

abnormal   anormal

abortion   aborto (*m.*)

about   sobre; unos(as); acerca de; como; (*with time*) a eso de

above   sobre
— **all**   sobre todo

absent   ausente

abuse   maltrato (*m.*); maltratar, abusar

accelerator   acelerador (*m.*)

accent   acento (*m.*)

accept   aceptar

accessory   accesorio (*m.*)

accident   accidente (*m.*)

accompany   acompañar

accomplice   cómplice (*m., f.*)

according to   de acuerdo con; según

accusation   acusación (*f.*), denuncia (*f.*)

accuse   denunciar, acusar

ache   doler (o:ue)

acid (LSD)   pegao (*m.*) (*coll.*)

acne   acné (*m.*)

acquaintance   conocido(a) (*m., f.*)

acquitted   absuelto(a)

across the street from   enfrente de
act   acto (*m.*); actuar
activity   actividad (*f.*)
addicted   adicto(a)
additional   adicional
address   dirección (*f.*), domicilio (*m.*)
   — book   libreta de direcciones (*f.*)
adhesive tape   cinta adhesiva (*f.*), esparadrapo
   (*m.*)
adjective   adjetivo (*m.*)
administrator   administrador(a) (*m., f.*)
admitted (to)   ingresado(a)
adolescent   adolescente (*m., f.*), jovencito(a)
   (*m., f.*)
adult   adulto(a) (*m., f.*); mayor de edad
advice   consejo (*m.*)
affair   cosa (*f.*)
affect   afectar
affirmative   afirmativo(a)
after   después (de)
afternoon   tarde (*f.*)
   in the —   por la tarde
afterward   después (de), luego
again   otra vez, de nuevo
against   en contra de, contra
age   edad (*f.*)
agency   agencia (*f.*)
aggression   agresión (*f.*)
aggressor   agresor(a) (*m., f.*)
ago: a month —   hace un mes
   a week —   hace una semana
agree   estar de acuerdo
agreement   acuerdo (*m.*)

aid ayuda (*f.*)
  **— to Families with Dependent Children
  (AFDC)** ayuda a familias con niños (*f.*)
AIDS SIDA (síndrome de inmunodeficiencia
  adquirida) (*m.*)
aim (a gun) apuntar
air conditioning aire acondicionado (*m.*)
alarm alarma (*f.*)
alcohol alcohol (*m.*)
alcoholic alcohólico(a)
Alcoholics Anonymous Alcohólicos Anónimos
alias alias (*m.*)
alibi coartada (*f.*)
alimony pensión alimenticia (*f.*)
all todo(a); todos(as); todo (*m.*)
  — day long todo el día
allergic alérgico(a)
allow dejar, autorizar
allowable permitido(a)
almost casi
alone solo(a)
alphabet abecedario (*m.*), alfabeto (*m.*)
already ya
also también
although aunque
always siempre
ambulance ambulancia (*f.*)
American (North American) americano(a),
  norteamericano(a)
among entre
amount cantidad (*f.*)
  small — pico (*m.*)
an un(a)
and y

angry enojado(a)
ankle tobillo (*m.*)
annoyed molesto(a)
another otro(a)
answer contestar; respuesta (*f.*), contestación (*f.*)
antibacterial antibacteriano(a)
antibiotic antibiótico (*m.*)
antidepressant antidepresivo (*m.*)
antihistamine antihistamínico (*m.*)
any algún(una), alguno; cualquier(a)
  — **one** cualquier(a)
  — **time** a sus órdenes
  not — ninguno(a)
anybody, **anyone** alguien, nadie
anything algo (*m.*), cualquier cosa (*f.*)
  — **else?** ¿Algo más?
  — **you say** cualquier cosa que diga
anyway de todos modos
apartment apartamento (*m.*)
appeal apelación (*f.*); apelar
appear aparecer, comparecer
  — **in court** comparecer ante un juez
applicant solicitante (*m.*, *f.*)
application solicitud (*f.*)
apply (for) solicitar, aplicar
  — **for aid** pedir (e:i) ayuda
appoint nombrar
appointment cita (*f.*), turno (*m.*)
approval aprobación (*f.*)
approximate aproximado(a)
approximately como, aproximadamente
area distrito (*m.*), área (*f.* but **el área**)
arm brazo (*m.*)

armchair sillón (*m.*)

around (approximately) unos(as)

arrange arreglar

arrangement arreglo (*m.*)

arrest arrestar, prender, detener, llevar preso(a)
   person under — detenido(a) (*m., f.*)

arrested arrestado(a), detenido(a), preso(a)

arrive (at) llegar (a)

arrow flecha (*f.*)

arson fuego intencional (*m.*), incendio
   intencional (*m.*)

arthritis artritis (*f.*)

article artículo (*m.*)

as como
   — (big, small, *etc.*) as tan (grande, pequeño,
    etc.) como
   — of a partir de
   — soon as en cuanto, tan pronto como
   — soon as possible lo más pronto posible,
    cuanto antes

Asian asiático(a)

ask (a question) preguntar
   — a favor pedir (e:i) un favor
   — a question hacer una pregunta
   — for solicitar, pedir (e:i)
   — to see . . . Solicite ver..., Pida ver...

asleep dormido(a)

assailant agresor(a) (*m., f.*), asaltante (*m., f.*)

assassin asesino(a) (*m., f.*)

assault asaltar; asalto (*m.*), agresión (*f.*), ataque
   (*m.*)

assembly reunión (*f.*), congregación (*f.*), mitin
   (*m.*)

asset propiedad (*f.*)

assigned asignado(a)
asthma asma (*f.* but **el asma**)
at en, a
— **dawn (daybreak)** al amanecer; de madrugada
— **dusk** al anochecer
— **home** en casa
— **least** por lo menos
— **midday** a (al) mediodía
— **midnight** a medianoche
— **night** por la noche
— **noon** a mediodía
— **present** ahora
— **the beginning** a partir de
— **the bottom of the page** al pie de la página
— **the end** al final
— **the moment** en este momento
— **this time (hour)** a esta hora
— **your service** para servir, a sus órdenes
attack atacar; ataque (*m.*), agresión (*f.*)
attempt intento (*m.*)
attend asistir (a)
aunt tía (*f.*)
authority autoridad (*f.*)
authorize autorizar
automatic automático(a)
automobile automóvil (*m.*)
autumn otoño (*m.*)
available disponible
avenue avenida (*f.*)
average mediano(a); promedio (*m.*)
avoid evitar

B

baby bebé (*m.*), bebito (*m.*)
   — bottle biberón (*m.*), mamadera (*f.*), mamila (*f.*) (*Méx.*)
   — carriage cochecito (*m.*)
   — food comidita de bebé (*f.*)
   — lotion loción para bebé (*f.*)
back (*of paper*) dorso (*m.*); (*part of body*) espalda (*f.*); (*adj.*) atrasado(a)
   in the — (of) en el fondo (de)
   on the — (of a page) al dorso
backyard patio (*m.*)
bad malo(a)
badly mal
bail fianza (*f.*)
   — bondsman fiancista (*m., f.*)
bailor fiancista (*m., f.*)
balance saldo (*m.*)
bald calvo(a), pelado(a), pelón(ona)
ball pelota (*f.*)
bandage venda (*f.*), vendaje (*m.*)
band-aid curita (*f.*)
bank banco (*m.*)
bankruptcy bancarrota (*f.*), quiebra (*f.*)
baptism certificate certificado de bautismo (*m.*), inscripción de bautismo (*f.*), partida de bautismo (*f.*), fe de bautismo (*f.*)
bar bar (*m.*), cantina (*f.*), barra (*f.*)
bargain ganga (*f.*)
basement sótano (*m.*)
basic básico(a)
bath baño (*m.*)
bathe bañarse

bathroom baño (*m.*), escusado (excusado) (*m.*)
   (*Méx.*)
bathtub bañadera (*f.*), bañera (*f.*) (*Puerto Rico*),
   tina (*f.*) (*Méx. y España*)
battery batería (*f.*), acumulador (*m.*)
be ser, estar
   — **able** poder (o:ue)
   — **about (+ *time*)** ser como las (+ *time*)
   — **acquainted with (a person, a
      place)** conocer
   — **admitted** ingresar
   — **afraid** temer, tener miedo
   — **at fault** tener la culpa (de), ser culpable
      (de)
   — **back** estar de vuelta, estar de regreso
   — **born** nacer
   — **called** llamarse
   — **careful** tener cuidado
   — **certain** estar seguro(a)
   — **(very) cold** hacer (mucho) frío
   — **embarrassed** darle vergüenza a uno
   — **enough** alcanzar
   — **free on bail (personal
      recognizance)** estar en libertad bajo
      fianza (palabra)
   — **free on probation** estar en libertad
      condicional
   — **glad** alegrarse (de)
   — **going to (do something)** ir a (+ *inf.*)
   — **guilty** tener la culpa (de), ser culpable (de)
   — **hereby declared illegal** quedar
      declarado(a) ilegal
   — **(very) hot** hacer (mucho) calor
   — **hungry** tener hambre

— **in a condition to (do something)** estar en condiciones de (+ *inf.*)
— **in a hurry** tener prisa
— **in charge (of)** encargarse (de), tener a su cargo
— **in jail** estar preso(a)
— **late** llegar tarde
— **located** quedar
— **lucky** tener suerte
— **missing** faltar
— **named** llamarse
— **nobody's business** no importarle a nadie
— **okay** estar bien
— **on the way** estar en camino
— **pleasing to** gustar
— **quiet!** ¡Cállese!
— **raised** criarse
— **right** tener razón
— **(very) sleepy** tener (mucho) sueño
— **(very) scared** tener (mucho) miedo
— **so scared** tener tanto miedo
— **(very) sunny** hacer (mucho) sol
— **(+ *amount*) tall** medir (e:i) (+ *amount*)
— **true** ser cierto
— **under arrest** darse preso(a); estar preso(a)
— **unemployed (out of work)** estar sin trabajo
— **visible** estar a la vista
— **(very) windy** hacer (mucho) viento
— **worth** valer
— **wrong** estar equivocado(a)
— **(+ *number*) years old** tener (+ *number*) años

beach playa (*f.*)

bear sobrellevar

beard barba (*f.*)

beat pegar

beating paliza (*f.*)

because porque

   — of por culpa de

become hacerse, convertirse (e:ie)

   — addicted to drugs endrogarse

   — aware of darse cuenta de

   — paralyzed (crippled) quedarse
     paralítico(a)

bed cama (*f.*)

bedroom cuarto (*m.*), dormitorio (*m.*),
   habitación (*f.*), recámara (*f.*) (*Méx.*)

beer cerveza (*f.*)

before (*adv.*) antes; (*prep.*) antes (de)

   — they question you antes de que lo
     interroguen

begin comenzar (e:ie), empezar (e:ie), iniciar

behave comportarse

behind atrasado(a); atrás

   — your back detrás de la espalda

believe creer

belongings pertenencias (*f. pl.*)

below debajo de

belt cinto (*m.*), cinturón (*m.*), correa (*f.*)

bend down agacharse

benefit beneficio (*m.*)

besides además (de)

best mejor

   the — thing (part) lo mejor

better mejor

   — than ever mejor que nunca

between entre
beverage bebida (*f.*)
bib babero (*m.*)
bicycle bicicleta (*f.*)
big grande
bilingual bilingüe
bill cuenta (*f.*)
birth nacimiento (*m.*)
  — **certificate** certificado de nacimiento (*m.*),
    inscripción de nacimiento (*f.*) (*Cuba*), partida
    de nacimiento (*f.*)
bit pico (*m.*)
bite mordida (*f.*)
black negro(a)
  — **heroin** negra (*f.*) (*coll.*)
blackmail chantaje (*m.*); chantajear
bladder stones cálculos en la vejiga (*m. pl.*)
blade arma blanca (*f.* but **el arma blanca**)
blame culpa (*f.*); culpar
blank space espacio en blanco (*m.*)
bleach lejía (*f.*)
bleed sangrar
blemish mancha (*f.*)
blind ciego(a)
blink parpadear
block cuadra (*f.*), manzana (*f.*); tapar
  a — from here a una cuadra de aquí
blond(e) rubio(a), güero(a) (*Méx.*)
blood sangre (*f.*)
  — **bank** banco de sangre (*m.*)
blouse blusa (*f.*)
blue azul
body cuerpo (*m.*); (*corpse*) cadáver (*m.*)
  — **hair** vello (*m.*)

bomb bomba (*f.*)

   time — bomba de tiempo (*f.*)

bond bono (*m.*)

book registrar, fichar

bookcase estante (*m.*)

bookstore librería (*f.*)

boot bota (*f.*)

borrow pedir (e:ie) prestado

boss patrón(ona) (*m., f.*), patrono (*m.*) (*Cuba*),
   jefe(a) (*m., f.*)

bothered molesto(a)

bottle botella (*f.*)

box cuadro (*m.*), cuadrado (*m.*)

boy muchacho (*m.*), chico (*m.*), chamaco (*m.*)

boyfriend novio (*m.*)

brake freno (*m.*)

brand marca (*f.*)

break descomponerse, romper

breast seno (*m.*)

breath aliento (*m.*)

breathe respirar

bribe soborno (*m.*)

brief breve

   — conversation conversación breve (*f.*)

bring traer

brochure folleto (*m.*)

broken down descompuesto(a)

broker's fee honorario de corredor (*m.*)

bronchitis bronquitis (*f.*)

brother hermano (*m.*)

   —-in-law cuñado (*m.*)

brown (hair, eyes) castaño(a), café

bruise moretón (*m.*), morado (*m.*), cardenal (*m.*)

buddy compañero(a) (*m., f.*)

bug-eyes (bulging eyes)   ojos saltones (*m. pl.*)

build   complexión (*f.*)

building   edificio (*m.*)

bullet   bala (*f.*)

bump (on the head)   chichón (*m.*)

burden   carga (*f.*)

burglar   ladrón(ona) (*m., f.*)

burglary   robo (*m.*)

burn (oneself)   quemar(se); quemadura (*f.*)

bus   ómnibus (*m.*), autobús (*m.*), guagua (*f.*) (*Cuba y Puerto Rico*)

— **station**   estación de ómnibus (autobuses) (*f.*)

— **stop**   parada de autobuses (*f.*), parada de guaguas (*f.*) (*Cuba y Puerto Rico*), parada de ómnibus (*f.*)

businessman(woman)   hombre (mujer) de negocios (*m., f.*)

busy   ocupado(a)

but   pero

butt in   entremeterse, entrometerse

butter   mantequilla (*f.*)

buttock   nalga (*f.*)

button   botón (*m.*)

buy   comprar

by   por

— **(the) hand**   de (la) mano

— **himself (herself)**   por sí mismo(a)

— **force**   a la fuerza

— **mail**   por correo

— **phone**   por teléfono

C

cab (of a truck) cabina (*f.*)
caliber calibre (*m.*)
call llamar; llamada (*f.*)
  — **off the dog** llamar al perro
calm quieto(a)
  — **down** calmarse
can poder (o:ue)
cancer cáncer (*m.*)
cane bastón (*m.*)
cannot: You (One) — write . . . No se puede escribir...
cap gorra (*f.*)
car auto(móvil) (*m.*), carro (*m.*), coche (*m.*), máquina (*f.*) (Cuba)
  — **-related** automovilístico(a)
carburetor carburador (*m.*)
card tarjeta (*f.*)
cardiogram cardiograma (*m.*)
care cuidado (*m.*)
Careful! ¡Cuidado!
carefully con cuidado
carpet alfombra (*f.*)
carry llevar
  — **out** realizar
case caso (*m.*)
  — **history** información sobre el caso (*f.*)
cash efectivo (*m.*)
  — **a check** cambiar (cobrar) un cheque
  — **register** caja (*f.*)
  in — en efectivo
cashier cajero(a) (*m., f.*)
cataracts cataratas (*f. pl.*)

Catholic católico(a)
caucasian blanco(a)
cause causar
 — **damage** perjudicar
ceiling techo (*m.*)
cell celda (*f.*)
cent centavo (*m.*), chavo (*m.*) (*Puerto Rico*)
central central
certain cierto(a)
Certainly! ¡Cómo no!
certificate certificado (*m.*), partida (*f.*)
 — **of deposit (CD)** certificado de depósito
  (*m.*)
chain cadena (*f.*)
chair silla (*f.*)
change cambio (*m.*); cambiar
 — **clothes** cambiarse de ropa
 — **into** convertirse (e:ie) en
 — **jobs** cambiar de trabajo
chapter capítulo (*m.*)
characteristic característica (*f.*)
charge acusación (*f.*); cobrar
cheap barato(a)
cheat engañar
check examinar, revisar, chequear; cheque (*m.*)
 — **off** marcar
checkbook talonario de cheques (*m.*), chequera
 (*f.*) (*Cuba y Puerto Rico*)
checking account cuenta corriente (*f.*), cuenta
 de cheques (*f.*)
cheek mejilla (*f.*), cachete (*m.*)
chemical químico(a)
chest pecho (*m.*)
 — **of drawers** cómoda (*f.*)

chickenpox   varicela (*f.*)
child   niño(a) (*m., f.*)
— **'s car seat**   asiento para el niño (*m.*)
— **care license**   licencia para cuidar niños (*f.*)
— **support**   pensión alimenticia (*f.*)
children   hijos (*m.*), chicos(as) (*m., f.*), niños(as) (*m., f.*)
— **'s Protection Department**   Sección Protectora de Niños (*f.*), Departamento de Protección de Niños (*m.*)
chin   barbilla (*f.*)
chiropractor   quiropráctico(a) (*m., f.*)
choose   escoger, elegir (e:i)
chosen   elegido(a)
Christmas   Navidad (*f.*)
church   iglesia (*f.*)
cigarette   cigarrillo (*m.*)
citizen   ciudadano(a) (*m., f.*)
citizenship   ciudadanía (*f.*)
city   ciudad (*f.*)
— **(housing) project**   proyecto de la ciudad (*m.*)
class   clase (*f.*), curso (*m.*)
classmate   compañero(a) de clase (*m., f.*)
clean   limpiar
cleaning   limpieza (*f.*)
clergy (person)   pastor(a) (*m., f.*)
clerk   empleado(a) (*m., f.*), dependiente (*m., f.*)
client   cliente(a) (*m., f.*)
climb   subir
clinic   clínica (*f.*)
close   cerrar (e:ie)
— **to**   cerca (de)
closed   cerrado(a)

closeted   encerrado(a)
clothes   ropa (*f.*)
clothing   ropa (*f.*)
clue   pista (*f.*)
clutch   embrague (*m.*)
coat   abrigo (*m.*)
cocaine   coca (*f.*), cocaína (*f.*); (*coll.*) perico (*m.*),
   polvo (*m.*)
cockroach   cucaracha (*f.*)
cognate   cognado (*m.*)
coin   moneda (*f.*)
cold   catarro (*m.*), resfrío (*m.*)
colic   cólico (*m.*)
colitis   colitis (*f.*)
collar   cuello (*m.*)
collect   cobrar
collide   chocar
collision   choque (*m.*)
color   color (*m.*)
comb   peine (*m.*)
come   venir (e:ie)
   — **back**   volver (o:ue), regresar
   — **from**   provenir (e:ie)
   — **in**   pasar, entrar (en)
   — **with**   acompañar
commission   comisión (*f.*)
commit   cometer
   — **suicide**   suicidarse
common   común
   — **-law marriage**   concubinato (*m.*)
cummunicate   comunicar
commute   ir y venir
compact disc   disco compacto (*m.*)
companion   compañero(a) (*m., f.*)

compassion compasión (*f.*)
complain protestar, quejarse
complaint queja (*f.*)
complete completo(a); completar
completely por completo
complication complicación (*f.*)
compulsory obligatorio(a)
computer computadora (*f.*), ordenador (*m.*)
  (*España*)
condition condición (*f.*)
condom condón (*m.*), preservativo (*m.*)
confess confesar (e:ie)
confession confesión (*f.*)
confidential confidencial
confirm confirmar
confused confuso(a)
consecutive consecutivo(a)
consent consentimiento (*m.*)
consider considerar
consist (of) consistir (en)
consulate consulado (*m.*)
consult consultar
contact contacto (*m.*)
  — lenses lentes de contacto (*m. pl.*)
contagious contagioso(a)
content contenido (*m.*)
continue seguir (e:i), continuar
contraband contrabando (*m.*)
contract contrato (*m.*)
control control (*m.*)
convalescent convaleciente (*m., f.*)
convenience conveniencia (*f.*)
conversation conversación (*f.*)
convict declarar culpable

convince   convencer
cook   cocinar; cocinero(a) (*m.*, *f.*)
  — **(prepare) dinner**   hacer la comida
cooperate   cooperar
cooperation   cooperación (*f.*)
copy   copia (*f.*)
corduroy   pana (*f.*)
corner   esquina (*f.*), rincón (*m.*)
corporal punishment   castigo corporal (*m.*)
correct   correcto(a)
cosmetics   cosméticos (*m. pl.*)
cost   costar (o:ue); costo (*m.*)
cough   tos (*f.*); toser
counsel for the defense   abogado(a) defensor(a) (*m.*, *f.*)
counselor   consejero(a) (*m.*, *f.*)
count   contar (o:ue)
counter   mostrador (*m.*)
counterfeit   falsificar; falsificación (*f.*)
country   campo (*m.*); (*nation*) país (*m.*)
  — **of origin**   país de origen (*m.*)
county   condado (*m.*)
couple   pareja (*f.*)
  a — **of**   un par de
course   curso (*m.*)
court (of law)   corte (*f.*), tribunal (*m.*), juzgado (*m.*)
  — **hearing**   vista (*f.*)
  — **reporter**   taquígrafo(a) (*m.*, *f.*)
courtesy   cortesía (*f.*)
courthouse   juzgado (*m.*); tribunal (*m.*)
cousin   primo(a) (*m.*, *f.*)
cover   cubrir, tapar
covered   cubierto(a)

crack cocaine   crac (*m.*); (*coll.*) piedra (*f.*), roca
    (*f.*), coca cocinada (*f.*)
crash   choque (*m.*)
crawl   gatear
cream   crema (*f.*)
credit card   tarjeta de crédito (*f.*)
crib   cuna (*f.*)
crime   crimen (*m.*), delito (*m.*)
criminal   criminal
    — record   antecedentes penales (*m. pl.*)
crippled   inválido(a), paralítico(a)
crisis   crisis (*f.*)
cross   cruzar; cruz (*f.*)
cross-eyed   bizco(a)
crossing   cruce (*m.*)
croup   crup (*m.*), garrotillo (*m.*)
crowbar   pata de cabra (*f.*)
crowd   multitud (*f.*)
cry   llorar
cultural   cultural
curfew   toque de queda (*m.*)
curly   rizado(a), rizo(a), crespo(a)
custody   custodia (*f.*)
customer   cliente (*m., f.*)
cut   cortadura (*f.*), cortada (*f.*) (*Méx. y Cuba*);
    cortar

D

dad   padre (*m.*), papá (*m.*)
dagger   puñal (*m.*), daga (*f.*)
daily   (*adv.*) al día, por día; (*adj.*) diario(a)
damage   desperfecto (*m.*)
danger   peligro (*m.*)

dangerous peligroso(a)
— **curve** curva peligrosa (*f.*)
dark oscuro(a)
data datos (*m. pl.*)
date fecha (*f.*); salir con
daughter hija (*f.*)
— **-in-law** nuera (*f.*)
day día (*m.*)
  during the — durante el día
  the — after tomorrow pasado mañana
  the — before yesterday anteayer, antes de
    ayer
deadbolt cerrojo de seguridad (*m.*)
deaf sordo(a)
death muerte (*f.*)
— **certificate** certificado de defunción (*m.*),
    inscripción de defunción (*f.*), partida de
    defunción (*f.*)
debt deuda (*f.*)
deceased fallecido(a)
deceive engañar
decide decidir
decision decisión (*f.*), fallo (*m.*)
deduct descontar (o:ue)
deductible deducible
deduction deducción (*f.*)
defend (oneself) defender(se)
defendant acusado(a) (*m., f.*), reo(a) (*m., f.*)
deform deformar
deformed deformado(a)
degree grado (*m.*)
deliver entregar
delivery entrega (*f.*)
demand exigir

den sala de estar (*f.*)
denied denegado(a)
dental dental
denture dentadura postiza (*f.*)
department departamento (*m.*)
depend depender
dependent dependiente (*m., f.*)
describe describir
description descripción (*f.*)
desk escritorio (*m.*)
destroy destruir
detail detalle (*m.*)
detain detener (e:ie)
detective detective (*m., f.*)
detention detención (*f.*)
detergent detergente (*m.*)
determine determinar
detour desvío (*m.*)
detoxification desintoxicación (*f.*)
diabetes diabetes (*f.*)
diagnosis diagnóstico (*m.*)
diaper pañal (*m.*)
diarrhea diarrea (*f.*)
die morir (o:ue), fallecer
different diferente
difficult difícil
difficulty dificultad (*f.*)
dining room comedor (*m.*)
dinner cena (*f.*)
diploma diploma (*m.*), título (*m.*)
directly directamente
dirty sucio(a)
disability incapacidad (*f.*), defecto físico (*m.*)
disabled inválido(a), paralítico(a)

disappear desaparecer

discharge (from the hospital) dar de alta

discipline disciplinar; disciplina (*f.*)

discrimination discriminación (*f.*)

discuss discutir

disease enfermedad (*f.*)

disfigured desfigurado(a)

dispatcher operador(a) (*m., f.*), telefonista (*m., f.*)

disperse dispersar(se)

disposable desechable

distribute distribuir

district barrio (*m.*), colonia (*f.*) (*Méx.*)

    — attorney fiscal (*m., f.*)

divided road doble vía (*f.*)

dividend dividendo (*m.*)

division división (*f.*), sección (*f.*)

divorce divorciarse

    — proceedings trámites de divorcio (*m. pl.*)

divorced divorciado(a)

dizzy mareado(a)

do hacer, realizar

do not no

    — enter. ¡No entre!

    — jump. ¡No salte!

    — litter ¡No tire basura!

    — mention it. No hay de qué.

    — move! ¡No se mueva!

    — pass. No pasar., No rebasar.

    — shoot! ¡No dispare!, ¡No tire!

doctor médico(a) (*m., f.*), doctor(a) (*m., f.*)

document documento (*m.*)

dollar dólar (*m.*)

domestic violence violencia doméstica (*f.*)

domicile domicilio (*m.*)

door puerta (*f.*)

double doble

doubt dudar

down payment enganche (*m.*) (*Méx.*), entrada (*f.*), inicial (*m.*)

downtown area centro (*m.*)

dress vestido (*m.*)

dressed vestido(a)

drink trago (*m.*), bebida (*f.*); tomar, beber

drinking bebida (*f.*)

drive manejar, conducir, guiar (*Puerto Rico*)
— **fifty miles per hour** conducir a cincuenta millas por hora
— **safely!** ¡Maneje con cuidado!

driver chofer (*m.*), conductor(a) (*m., f.*)
—**'s license** licencia para manejar (*f.*), licencia de conducir (*f.*)

drop saltar (o:ue)
— **out of school** abandonar los estudios
— **the gun (weapon)** soltar el arma

drown ahogarse

drug droga (*f.*)
— **addict** drogadicto(a) (*m., f.*)
— **pusher** droguero(a) (*m., f.*)
— **user** droguero(a) (*m., f.*)
on drugs endrogado(a)

drunk driving manejar estando borracho(a)

dry seco(a)

due to por
— **illness** por enfermedad

during durante

dynamite dinamita (*f.*)

E

each cada
ear (*inner*) oído (*m.*), (*outer*) oreja (*f.*)
early temprano
earn ganar
earnings ganancias (*f. pl.*), ingresos (*m. pl.*)
earring arete (*m.*)
earthquake terremoto (*m.*)
east este (*m.*)
easy fácil
eat comer
either cualquier(a), tampoco
elbow codo (*m.*)
elderly man (woman) anciano(a) (*m., f.*)
electric(al) eléctrico(a)
  — **appliance** aparato eléctrico (*m.*), (equipo) electrodoméstico (*m.*)
  — **outlet** tomacorrientes (*m. sing.*), enchufe (*m.*)
electricity electricidad (*f.*)
eligibility elegibilidad (*f.*)
eligible elegible
emergency emergencia (*f.*)
  — **parking only** estacionamiento de emergencia solamente
  — **room** sala de emergencia (*f.*)
employee empleado(a) (*m., f.*)
empty desocupado(a); vaciar
end final (*m.*), punta (*f.*); terminar
endanger poner en peligro
engine motor (*m.*)
English (language) inglés (*m.*)
enough (lo) suficiente

enroll (in a school) matricularse
enter entrar (en), ingresar
  do not — no entre; no pase
entrance entrada (f.)
epidemic epidemia (f.)
epileptic epiléptico(a)
equipment equipo (m.)
especially sobre todo
establish establecer
estimate estimado (m.)
even though aunque
evening noche (f.)
  in the — por la noche
ever alguna vez
every cada, todos(as)
  — day todos los días
everything todo (m.)
  — possible todo lo posible
eviction desalojo (m.)
evidence evidencia (f.), prueba (f.)
ex ex
exactly exactamente
examination examen (m.)
examine examinar, chequear
example ejemplo (m.)
  for — por ejemplo
excessive demasiado(a)
excuse excusa (f.)
  — me perdón
exempt exento(a)
exit salida (f.)
  — door puerta de salida (f.)
expense gasto (m.)
expensive caro(a)

expert   perito(a) (*m., f.*)
expire   vencer
explain   explicar
explosive   explosivo (*m.*)
expression   expresión (*f.*)
  — **of courtesy**   expresión de cortesía (*f.*)
extend credit   conceder un crédito
extent: to a large —   en buena parte
extra   extra
eye   ojo (*m.*)
  — **examination**   examen de la vista (*m.*)
  with (blue) eyes   de ojos (azules)
eyebrow   ceja (*f.*)
eyeglasses   anteojos (*m.*), lentes (*m.*), espejuelos
  (*m.*) (*Cuba y Puerto Rico*), gafas (*f.*)
eyelashes   pestañas (*f. pl.*)

F

face   cara (*f.*)
  — **down**   boca abajo
  — **up**   boca arriba
factory   fábrica (*f.*), factoría (*f.*)
fair   justo(a)
fake   falso(a)
  — **identification**   identificación falsa (*f.*)
  — **statement**   declaración falsa (*f.*)
fall   caerse; (*season*) otoño
  — **ill**   enfermarse
falsification   falsificación (*f.*)
falsify   falsificar
family   familia (*f.*)
  — **counselor**   consejero(a) familiar (*m., f.*)
  — **room**   sala de estar (*f.*)

— **tension** tensión familiar (*f.*)

far lejos

— **from** lejos de

farewell despedida (*f.*)

farm worker trabajador(a) agrícola (*m., f.*)

fast rápido

fat gordo(a), grueso(a)

father padre (*m.*), papá (*m.*)

— **-in-law** suegro (*m.*)

fear temer

federal federal

feed alimentar, dar de comer, amamantar

feel sentir(se) (e:ie)

— **sorry** arrepentirse (e:ie)

felony delito mayor (*m.*), delito grave (*m.*)

fender guardafangos (*m.*)

fever fiebre (*f.*), calentura (*f.*)

few pocos(as)

fewer than menos de

fiancé(e) prometido(a) (*m., f.*)

field campo (*m.*)

fight luchar; pelea (*f.*), riña (*f.*)

file presentar

— **an appeal** presentar una apelación

— **a law suit** presentar una demanda

fill out llenar

filter filtro (*m.*)

finally ya

finances finanzas (*f. pl.*)

financial económico(a)

— **assistance** ayuda en dinero (*f.*)

find encontrar (o:ue), hallar

— **out** averiguar, enterarse

— **refuge (shelter)** refugiarse

fine *(adv.)* bien; multa *(f.)*
   —, thank you. And you?   Bien, gracias. ¿Y
     Ud.?
finger   dedo *(m.)*
fingerprint   huella digital *(f.)*; tomar las huellas
   digitales
finish   terminar
   — (doing something)   terminar de (+ *inf.*)
fire   fuego *(m.)*, incendio *(m.)*; *(from a job)*
   despedir (e:i), cesantear
   — department   estación de bomberos *(f.)*
   — extinguisher   extinguidor de incendios
     (m.), extintor de incendios *(m.)* *(España)*
   — fighter   bombero(a) *(m., f.)*
firearm   arma de fuego *(f.* but **el arma de fuego)**
first   *(adj.)* primero(a); *(adv.)* primero
   — aid   primeros auxilios *(m. pl.)*
   — aid kit   estuche de primeros auxilios *(m.)*,
     botiquín de primeros auxilios *(m.)*
   — class   de primera calidad
   — name   nombre de pila *(m.)*
   the — thing   lo primero
fist   puño *(m.)*
fix   arreglar
fixed   fijo(a)
flashlight   linterna *(f.)*
flat tire   goma ponchada *(f.)*, llanta pinchada *(f.)*
floor   piso *(m.)*
flower   flor *(f.)*
   — pot   maceta de flores *(f.)*
flowered   floreado(a)
flu   influenza *(f.)*, gripe *(f.)*
fog   niebla *(f.)*, nieblina *(f.)*
follow   seguir (e:i)

following siguiente
  the — lo siguiente
  the — day al día siguiente
food alimento (*m.*), comida (*f.*)
  — stamp estampilla para alimento (*f.*), cupón para comida (*m.*)
foolishness tontería (*f.*)
foot pie (*m.*)
  — print huella (*f.*)
for para, por
  — a while por un tiempo
  — example por ejemplo
  — me por mí, para mí
  — possession of drugs por poseer drogas
  — that reason por eso
  — today para hoy mismo
  — what reason? ¿para qué?
  — you para ti
forbid prohibir
forbidden prohibido(a)
force forzar (o:ue), obligar; fuerza (*f.*)
  by — a la fuerza
forehead frente (*f.*)
foreign extranjero(a)
foreigner extranjero(a) (*m., f.*)
forge falsificar
forged falso(a)
  — document documento falso (*m.*)
forgery falsificación (*f.*)
forget olvidarse (de)
forgive perdonar
forgiveness perdón (*m.*)
form papeleta (*f.*), planilla (*f.*), forma (*f.*)
former ex

formula fórmula (*f.*)

fortunately por suerte

foster: — child hijo(a) de crianza (*m., f.*)

— **home** hogar de crianza (*m.*), hogar sustituto (*m.*)

— **parents** padres de crianza (*m. pl.*)

fourth cuarto(a)

fracture fractura (*f.*)

fraud estafa (*f.*)

freckle peca (*f.*)

free (of charge) (*adv.*) gratis; (*adj.*) gratuito(a)

— **service** servicio gratuito (*m.*)

— **time** rato libre (*m.*), tiempo libre (*m.*)

Freeze! ¡Quieto(a)!, ¡No se mueva(n)!

frequently frecuentemente

fresh nuevo(a)

friend amigo(a) (*m., f.*)

frightened aterrorizado(a)

from de, desde

front: in — of frente a

— **door** puerta de la calle (*f.*)

frustrated frustrado(a)

fuel combustible (*m.*)

full time tiempo completo

funeral expenses gastos funerarios (*m. pl.*)

fur coat abrigo de piel (*m.*)

furniture muebles (*m. pl.*)

further más

future futuro (*m.*)

G

gag mordaza (*f.*)

gain ganancia (*f.*); ganar

gallstones cálculos en la vesícula (*m. pl.*)
gang pandilla (*f.*)
garage garaje (*m.*)
garbage basura (*f.*)
garden jardín (*m.*)
gardener jardinero(a) (*m., f.*)
gas gas (*m.*)
  — **pedal** acelerador (*m.*)
  — **station** gasolinera (*f.*), estación de servicio
    (*f.*)
gasoline gasolina (*f.*)
gauze gasa (*f.*)
gearshift cambio de velocidades (*m.*)
  — **lever** palanca de cambio de velocidades
    (*f.*), embrague (*m.*)
generally generalmente
gentleman señor (Sr.) (*m.*)
get conseguir (e:i), obtener
  — **along well** llevarse bien
  — **away** alejarse
  — **better** mejorarse
  — **down** bajarse
  — **drunk** emborracharse
  — **even with** desquitar(se)
  — **hold of** agarrar, coger
  — **hurt** lastimarse
  — **in (a car, etc.)** subir
  — **in touch** ponerse en contacto
  — **married** casarse (con)
  — **off** bajarse
  — **on one's knees** ponerse de rodillas
  — **out** salir, bajarse
  — **paid** cobrar
  — **sick** enfermarse

— **up** levantarse
— **well soon!** ¡Que se mejore!
— **worse** agravarse
gift regalo (*m.*)
girl muchacha (*f.*)
girlfriend novia (*f.*)
give dar, entregar
— **a gift** regalar
— **a fine (ticket)** imponer una multa
— **birth** dar a luz, parir
— **CPR** dar respiración artificial
— **notice** avisar de
Gladly! ¡Cómo no!
glass vidrio (*m.*)
— **cutter** cortavidrios (*m.*)
— **eye** ojo de vidrio (*m.*)
glove guante (*m.*)
— **compartment** guantera (*f.*), portaguantes
(*m.*)
go ir
— **around** andar
— **away** irse
— **in** entrar (en)
— **out** salir
— **through** atravesar (e:ie)
— **through a red light** pasarse la luz roja
— **up** subir
— **with** acompañar
God grant ojalá, Dios quiera
goddaughter ahijada (*f.*)
godfather padrino (*m.*), compadre (*m.*)
godmother madrina (*f.*), comadre (*f.*)
godson ahijado (*m.*)
gold oro (*m.*)

gonorrhea   gonorrea (*f.*)
good   bueno(a)
   — **afternoon.**   Buenas tardes.
   — **evening.**   Buenas noches.
   — **morning (day).**   Buenos días.
   — **night.**   Buenas noches.
   It's a — **thing!**   ¡Qué suerte!
good-bye   adiós
grab   agarrar, coger
grade   grado (*m.*)
   — **school**   escuela primaria (*f.*), escuela
   elemental (*f.*)
graffiti   grafiti (*m.*)
granddaughter   nieta (*f.*)
grandfather   abuelo (*m.*)
grandmother   abuela (*f.*)
grandson   nieto (*m.*)
gray   gris
gray-haired   canoso(a)
great   gran
green   verde
greet   saludar
greeting   saludo (*m.*)
gross earnings   entrada bruta (*f.*)
ground   suelo (*m.*)
group   grupo (*m.*)
guardian   tutor(a) (*m., f.*)
guilty   culpable

H

hair   pelo (*m.*), cabello (*m.*)
   body —   vello (*m.*)
hairpiece   peluca (*f.*)

hairy velludo(a)
half mitad (*f.*); (*adj.*) medio(a)
   — brother (sister) medio(a) hermano(a)
   (*m., f.*)
   — an hour media hora (*f.*)
hall pasillo (*m.*)
hallucinations alucinaciones (*f. pl.*)
Halt! ¡Alto!
hand mano (*f.*)
   — grenade granada de mano (*f.*)
handcuffed esposado(a)
handcuffs esposas (*f. pl.*)
handicapped incapacitado(a)
handkerchief pañuelo (*m.*)
handsaw sierra de mano (*f.*), serrucho de mano
   (*m.*)
happen pasar, suceder, ocurrir
hard duro(a)
hashish hachich (*m.*), hachís (*m.*); (*coll.*)
   chocolate (*m.*), kif (*m.*), grifa (*f.*)
hat gorro (*m.*), sombrero (*m.*)
have tener
   — a good time pasarlo bien, pasar un buen
    rato
   — a seat tomar asiento
   — good weather hacer buen tiempo
   — just (done something) acabar de (+ *inf.*)
   — on tener puesto(a), llevar puesto(a)
   — (something) fixed hacer arreglar
   — surgery operarse
   — the right to tener derecho a
   — to (do something) tener que (+ *inf.*)
   — worked haber trabajado
head cabeza (*f.*)

— of household jefe(a) de familia (*m., f.*), cabeza de la familia (*m., f.*)

headlight faro (*m.*)

health salud (*f.*)
— **Department** Departamento de Sanidad (*m.*)
— **insurance** seguro de salud (*m.*), aseguranza de salud (*f.*) (*Méx.*)
To your —! ¡Salud!

hear oír

hearing (court) audiencia (*f.*), vista (*f.*)
— **aid** audífono (*m.*)
— **test** examen del oído (*m.*)

heart corazón (*m.*)
— **attack** ataque al corazón (*m.*)

heat calefacción (*f.*)

heater calentador (*m.*), calentón (*m.*) (*Méx.*), estufa (*f.*)

heel talón (*m.*)

height estatura (*f.*)
of medium — de estatura mediana

helicopter helicóptero (*m.*)

hello hola; (*on the telephone*) Aló. (*Puerto Rico*), Bueno. (*Méx.*), Diga. (*Cuba y España*), Mande. (*Méx.*), Oigo. (*Cuba*)

helmet casco de seguridad (*m.*)

help ayuda (*f.*); ayudar
—! ¡Socorro!, ¡Auxilio!

hepatitis hepatitis (*f.*)

her su(s)

here aquí
— **is** aquí tiene
— **it is.** Aquí está.

heroin heroína (*f.*); (*coll.*) caballo (*m.*), manteca
    (*f.*) (*Caribe*), chiva (*f.*)
herpes herpe(s) (*m.*)
herself: by — por sí misma
hi hola
high alto(a)
   — blood pressure hipertensión (*f.*), presión
     alta (*f.*)
   — school escuela secundaria (*f.*)
highway autopista (*f.*), carretera (*f.*)
hijack asaltar
hijacking asalto (*m.*)
him lo
himself: by — por sí mismo
hip cadera (*f.*)
his su(s)
Hispanic hispano(a), hispánico(a), latino(a)
hit chocar, pegar, golpear, dar golpes
hold-up asalto (*m.*)
hole agujerito (*m.*)
holiday día feriado (*m.*), día de fiesta (*m.*)
home casa (*f.*), vivienda (*f.*)
   — for the elderly asilo de ancianos (*m.*),
     casa para ancianos (*f.*)
homeless desalojado(a), sin hogar
home(ward) a casa
homicide homicidio (*m.*)
honk the horn tocar la bocina
hood capucha (*f.*); (*car*) capó (*m.*); cubierta (*f.*)
hope esperar
   I — ojalá, Dios quiera
horn bocina (*f.*)
hospital hospital (*m.*), clínica (*f.*); policlínica (*f.*)
   — insurance seguro de hospitalización (*m.*)

hospitalization hospitalización (*f.*)
hospitalized hospitalizado(a)
hot caliente
hotel hotel (*m.*)
hour hora (*f.*)
house casa (*f.*)
household: — expenses gastos de la casa (*m. pl.*)
   — appliance aparato eléctrico (*m.*), (equipo) electrodoméstico (*m.*)
housekeeping quehaceres del hogar (de la casa) (*m. pl.*)
housewife ama de casa (*f.* but **el ama**)
housework trabajo de la casa (*m.*), tareas de la casa (*f. pl.*), quehaceres del hogar (de la casa) (*m. pl.*)
how? ¿cómo?
   — are you? ¿Cómo está usted?
   — do you spell it? ¿Cómo se escribe?
   — fortunate! ¡Qué suerte!
   — frequently? ¿Con qué frecuencia?
   — is it going? ¿Qué tal?
   — long? ¿cuánto tiempo?
   — long had . . . ? ¿Cuánto tiempo hacía que... ?
   — long have . . . ? ¿Cuánto tiempo hace que... ?
   — many? ¿cuántos(as)?
   — may I help you? ¿En qué puedo servirle?
   — much? ¿cuánto(a)?
   — much do you pay in rent? ¿Cuánto paga de alquiler?
   — often? ¿Con qué frecuencia?

— **old are you?**   ¿Cuántos años tiene Ud.?,
¿Qué edad tiene?

however   sin embargo

human immunodeficiency virus (HIV)   virus
de inmunodeficiencia humana (VIH) (*m.*)

humiliate   humillar

hurt   herido(a), lastimado(a); doler (o:ue),
perjudicar, causarle daño a
— **oneself**   lastimarse

husband   esposo (*m.*), marido (*m.*)

hydrogen peroxide   agua oxigenada (*f.* but **el
agua oxigenada**)

hypertension   hipertensión (*f.*), presión alta (*f.*)

hypodermic syringe   jeringuilla (*f.*), jeringa
hipodérmica (*f.*)

hysterical   histérico(a)

hysterically   histéricamente

I

ice   hielo (*m.*)

ID   identificación (*f.*)

idea   idea (*f.*)

identification   identificación (*f.*)

identify   identificar

if   si
— **possible**   si es posible

I'll see you tomorrow.   Hasta mañana.

ill   enfermo(a)

illegal immigrant   inmigrante ilegal,
indocumentado(a) (*m., f.*)

immediately   inmediatamente

immigrant   inmigración (*f.*)
— **card**   tarjeta de inmigración (*f.*)

immunize vacunar
imperfection desperfecto (*m.*)
important importante
impose a fine imponer una multa
impossible imposible
improve mejorar
imprudently imprudentemente
in en, dentro (de)
    — **addition to** además de
    — **case of** en caso de
    — **charge of** a cargo de
    — **front of** a la vista de
    — **installments** a plazos
    — **order to** para
    — **self-defense** en defensa propia
    — **that case** en ese caso
    — **the afternoon** por (de) la tarde
    — **the evening** por (de) la noche
    — **the first place** en primer lugar
    — **the morning** por (de) la mañana
    — **the presence of** a la vista de
    — **these situations** en estas situaciones
    — **this way** de este modo
    — **use** en uso
    — **writing** por escrito
incapacitated incapacitado(a)
incest incesto (*m.*)
inch pulgada (*f.*)
include incluir
including incluido(a)
income entrada (*f.*), ingreso (*m.*)
    — **tax** impuesto sobre la renta (*m.*)
increments of . . . dollars partidas de... dólares
    (*f. pl.*)

independent   independiente
index (finger)   (dedo) índice (*m.*)
indicted   procesado(a)
inexpensive   barato(a)
infect   infectar
infiltrate   infiltrar
inform   avisar de, notificar, informar
information   información (*f.*), datos (*m. pl.*)
   personal —   dato personal (*m.*)
inheritance   herencia (*f.*)
initial   inicial (*f.*)
initiate   iniciar
injured   herido(a), lastimado(a), lesionado(a)
injury   lesión (*f.*)
ink   tinta (*f.*)
in-laws   parientes políticos (*m. pl.*)
innocent   inocente
inpatient   paciente interno(a) (*m., f.*)
insecticide   insecticida (*m.*)
inserted in   metido(a)
inside   dentro, adentro, metido(a)
install   instalar
installment   plazo (*m.*)
   in —s   a plazos
instead of   en lugar de
insurance   seguro (*m.*), aseguranza (*f.*) (*Méx.*)
insured   asegurado(a)
intensive   intensivo(a)
interest   interés (*m.*)
interlace   entrelazar
interpreter   intérprete (*m., f.*)
interrogate   interrogar
interrogation   interrogatorio (*m.*)
intertwine   entrelazar

interview   entrevista (*f.*); entrevistar
introduce   presentar
investigate   investigar
investigating   investigador(a)
investigation   averiguación (*f.*), investigación (*f.*)
investment   inversión (*f.*)
ipecac   ipecacuana (*f.*)
iron   plancha (*f.*)
irritation   irritación (*f.*)
it   lo
   — **doesn't matter.**   No importa.
   — **may be**   puede ser
   —**'s (+ *time*)**   son las (+ *time*)
   —**'s nobody's business.**   A nadie le importa.
   —**'s not that way.**   No es así.
item   objeto (*m.*)

J

jack   gato (*m.*), gata (*f.*) (*Costa Rica y España*)
jacket   chaqueta (*f.*), chamarra (*f.*) (*Méx.*), saco (*m.*)
jail   cárcel (*f.*), prisión (*f.*)
jewelry   joya (*f.*)
   — **store**   joyería (*f.*)
Jewish   judío(a), hebreo(a)
job   trabajo (*m.*), empleo (*m.*)
jobless   desocupado(a)
joint   (*coll.*) cucaracha (*f.*), leño (*m.*), porro (*m.*)
judge   juez (*m., f.*); juzgar (a)
jump   saltar
junior high school   escuela secundaria (*f.*)
jury   jurado (*m.*)

just nada más que, no más que
  It's — that . . . Es que...
  — in time a tiempo
juvenile juvenil
  — court tribunal de menores (*m.*)
  — delinquent delincuente juvenil (*m., f.*)
  — hall centro de reclusión de menores (*m.*)

K

keep guardar, mantener (e:ie), quedarse con
  — right conserve su derecha, mantenga su
    derecha
  — walking seguir (e:i) caminando
key llave (*f.*)
kick patada (*f.*)
kidnap secuestrar
kidnapping secuestro (*m.*)
kidney riñón (*m.*)
kill matar
kind clase (*f.*)
kitchen cocina (*f.*)
knee rodilla (*f.*)
knife cuchillo (*m.*)
knock at the door tocar a la puerta
know conocer, (*something*) saber
  I —. Lo sé.

L

laboratory laboratorio (*m.*)
laborer obrero(a) (*m., f.*)
ladder escalera (*f.*)
  hand — escalera de mano (*f.*)

    rope — escalera de soga (*f.*)
lady señora (*f.*)
lame cojo(a)
lamp lámpara (*f.*)
landlord (lady) dueño(a) de la casa (*m., f.*)
lane carril (*m.*)
language idioma (*m.*), lengua (*f.*)
large grande
last durar
    at — ya
    — month el mes pasado
    — name apellido (*m.*)
    — night anoche
    — week la semana pasada
    — year el año pasado
late tarde
lately últimamente
later más tarde, después, luego
Latin latino(a)
law ley (*f.*)
lawn césped (*m.*), zacate (*m.*) (*Méx.*)
lawsuit demanda (*f.*)
lawyer abogado(a) (*m., f.*)
learn aprender
leave salir, irse
    — behind dejar
    — turned on dejar encendido(a), dejar
    prendido(a)
left izquierda (*f.*)
    — -handed zurdo(a)
    to the — a la izquierda
leg pierna (*f.*)
legal legal
lend prestar

less menos
— **... than** menos... que
— **than (*number*)** menos de (*number*)
let dejar
— **go of** soltar (o:ue)
— **(someone) know** avisar, hacer saber
let's (do something) vamos a (+ *inf.*)
— **go.** Vamos.
— **see** a ver
letter carta (*f.*)
license licencia (*f.*)
— **plate** placa (*f.*), chapa (*f.*)
lie mentira (*f.*); mentir (e:ie)
— **down** acostarse (o:ue)
life vida (*f.*)
— **insurance** seguro de vida (*m.*)
lift levantar
light luz (*f.*), foco (*m.*); (*light in color*) claro(a)
like como; gustar
— **that** así
limit límite (*m.*)
limited limitado(a)
line (on a paper or form) línea (*f.*), renglón (*m.*)
lip labio (*m.*)
liquid líquido (*m.*)
liquor store licorería (*f.*)
lisp hablar con (la) zeta
list lista (*f.*)
lit prendido(a)
little (*adv.*) poco; (*adj.*) poco(a); (*size*)
    pequeño(a); (*quantity*) poco (*m.*)
    a — un poco de
— **finger** meñique (*m.*)
live vivir

liver hígado (*m.*)

living room sala (*f.*)

loan préstamo (*m.*)

local local

lock cerradura (*f.*), cerrojo (*m.*); cerrar (e:ie) con llave

— **up** encerrar (e:ie)

locked cerrado(a)

— **up** encerrado(a)

lodging alojamiento (*m.*), hospedaje (*m.*), vivienda (*f.*)

log in registrar, fichar

long largo(a)

— **-sleeved** de mangas largas

— **-term** a plazo largo

look (*at*) mirar, (*for*) buscar

Look. Mire.

What does he/she (do you) — like? ¿Cómo es?

lose perder (e:ie)

— **one's job** quedarse sin trabajo

loss pérdida (*f.*)

lost perdido(a)

low bajo(a)

— **-income** (de) bajos ingresos

LSD ácido (*m.*); (*coll.*) pastilla (*f.*), pegao (*m.*), sello (*m.*)

luck suerte (*f.*)

What —! ¡Qué suerte!

luckily por suerte

luego later

lunch almuerzo (*m.*)

lung pulmón (*m.*)

M

Ma'am señora (Sra.) (*f.*)
machine gun ametralladora (*f.*)
Madam señora (Sra.) (*f.*)
magazine revista (*f.*)
maiden name apellido de soltera (*m.*)
mail correo (*m.*), correspondencia (*f.*)
main principal
majority mayoría (*f.*)
make hacer; (*car*) marca (*f.*)
   — a decision tomar una decisión
   — a false statement hacer una declaración
      falsa
   — violent poner violento(a)
male chauvinism machismo (*m.*)
man hombre (*m.*)
manage conseguir (e:i)
manslaughter homicidio (*m.*)
many muchos(as)
   — thanks. Muchas gracias.
   — times muchas veces
marijuana mariguana (*f.*), marihuana (*f.*),
   marijuana (*f.*); (*coll.*) mota (*f.*), pasto (*m.*), pito
   (*m.*), zacate (*m.*), yerba (*f.*), yesca (*f.*), juanita (*f.*)
marital status estado civil (*m.*)
mark marca (*f.*), mancha (*f.*); marcar
market mercado (*m.*)
   open-air — mercado al aire libre (*m.*),
      tianguis (*m.*) (*Méx.*)
marriage matrimonio (*m.*)
   — certificate certificado de matrimonio (*m.*),
      inscripción de matrimonio, (*f.*), partida de
      matrimonio (*f.*)

married casado(a)

marry casarse (con)

mask máscara (f.)

mat felpudo (m.)

match fósforo (m.)

matter importar

 It doesn't —. No importa.

 What's the — with you? ¿Qué te pasa?

mature madurar

may: it — be . . . puede ser...

maybe a lo mejor, quizá(s)

meal comida (f.)

mean querer (e:ie) decir, significar

meantime: in the — mientras tanto

measles sarampión (m.)

measure medir (e:i)

mechanic mecánico (m.)

meddle entremeterse, entrometerse

medical médico(a)

 — history historia clínica (f.)

 — insurance seguro médico (m.)

medication medicina (f.), medicamento (m.)

medicine medicina (f.)

medium mediano(a)

 — height (de) estatura mediana

meeting reunión (f.), congregación (f.), mitin (m.), junta (f.)

member miembro (m., f.)

mention: Don't — it. De nada., No hay de qué.

message mensaje (m.)

methadone metadona (f.)

middle medio (m.)

 about the — of the month (week) a mediados de mes (semana)

— **finger** dedo mayor (*m.*), dedo (del) corazón (*m.*)

— **name** segundo nombre (*m.*)

midnight medianoche (*f.*)

mile milla (*f.*)

milk leche (*f.*)

minor menor de edad (*m., f.*), menor

minute minuto (*m.*)

Miranda Warning advertencia Miranda (*f.*)

mirror espejo (*m.*)

misbehave portarse mal

mischief travesura (*f.*)

mischievous travieso(a), majadero(a), juguetón(ona)

misdemeanor delito (*m.*)

Miss señorita (Srta.) (*f.*)

miss faltar

— **class** faltar a clase

missing desaparecido(a)

mistreat maltratar

mixed race (*black and white*) mulato(a); (*any of two or more races*) mestizo(a)

mobile home casa rodante (*f.*)

model modelo (*m.*)

molar muela (*f.*)

mole lunar (*m.*)

mom mamá (*f.*), madre (*f.*)

moment momento (*m.*)

money dinero (*m.*)

month mes (*m.*)

a — **ago** hace un mes

monthly mensual, al mes

monument monumento (*m.*)

more más

— **or less** más o menos

— **... than** más... que

— **than** (*number*) más de (*number*)

— **than ever** más que nunca

morgue morgue (*f.*)

morning mañana (*f.*)

  early — madrugada (*f.*)

  in the — por la mañana

morphine morfina (*f.*)

mortgage hipoteca (*f.*)

most important thing lo más importante

motel motel (*m.*)

mother madre (*f.*), mamá (*f.*)

  — **-in-law** suegra (*f.*)

motive motivo (*m.*)

motor motor (*m.*)

motorcycle motocicleta (*f.*)

mouse ratón (*m.*)

moustache bigote (*m.*)

mouth boca (*f.*)

move moverse (o:ue), (*to another lodging*)

  mudarse

  Don't —! ¡No se mueva(n)!

movie theatre cine (*m.*)

movies cine (*m.*)

moving (to another lodging) mudanza (*f.*)

mow cortar

Mr. señor (Sr.) (*m.*)

  — **and Mrs. (Ruiz)** los señores (Ruiz) (*m. pl.*)

Mrs. señora (Sra.) (*f.*)

much (*adv.*) mucho

mud barro (*m.*), fango (*m.*)

muffler silenciador (*m.*), amortiguador de ruido (*m.*)

mug asaltar
mugging asalto (*m.*)
mumps paperas (*f. pl.*)
municipal municipal
murder asesinar; asesinato (*m.*)
murderer asesino(a) (*m., f.*)
murmur murmurar
muscular musculoso(a)
must (do something) deber (+ *inf.*)
mute mudo(a)
mutual fund fondo mutuo (*m.*)
my mi(s)
myself yo mismo(a)

N

nanny niñera (*f.*)
name nombre (*m.*)
nationality nacionalidad (*f.*)
natural healer curandero(a) (*m., f.*)
near cercano(a); (*prep.*) cerca de
nearby cercano(a)
necessary necesario(a)
neck cuello (*m.*)
necklace collar (*m.*)
need necesitar, hacer falta; necesidad (*f.*)
needle aguja (*f.*)
negative negativo(a)
neglect descuidar
neighbor vecino(a) (*m., f.*)
neighborhood barrio (*m.*), colonia (*f.*) (*Méx.*),
   vecindario (*m.*)
   — watch vigilancia del barrio (*f.*)
neither . . . nor ni... ni

nephew   sobrino (*m.*)
nervous depression   depresión nerviosa (*f.*)
net   neto(a)
   — income   entrada neta (*f.*)
never   nunca
   — before   nunca antes
nevertheless   sin embargo
new   nuevo(a)
newborn baby   recién nacido(a) (*m., f.*)
newspaper   periódico (*m.*), diario (*m.*)
next   próximo(a), siguiente
   — door   de al lado
   — month   el mes que viene, el mes próximo
   — week   la semana que viene, la semana
     próxima
   the — day   al día siguiente
niece   sobrina (*f.*)
night   noche (*f.*)
   — school   escuela nocturna (*f.*)
   — table   mesita de noche (*f.*)
   the — before last   anteanoche, antes de
     anoche
no   no, ningún(una)
   — longer   ya no
nobody   nadie
noise   ruido (*m.*)
nonsense   tontería (*f.*)
north   norte (*m.*)
northeast   noreste (*m.*)
northwest   noroeste (*m.*)
nose   nariz (*f.*)
not   no
   — a cent   ni un centavo
   — any   ningún(a)

— **at the present time** ahora no
— **go well** no andar bien
— **now** ahora no
note nota (*f.*)
  take — of anotar
nothing nada
notice notar
notify avisar, notificar
noun nombre (*m.*)
now ahora, ahorita (*Méx.*)
number número (*m.*)
numbered numerado(a)
nurse (a baby) dar el pecho, amamantar
  —'s aide auxiliar de enfermera (*m., f.*)
nursery school guardería (*f.*), centro de cuidado
  de niños (*m.*) (*Puerto Rico*)

O

oath juramento (*m.*)
  to take an — jurar
  under — bajo juramento
object objeto (*m.*)
obligate obligar
obscenity obscenidad (*f.*)
observe observar
obtain obtener
occasion ocasión (*f.*)
occur ocurrir
of de
  — age mayor de edad
  — course desde luego, claro que sí
off (light) apagado(a)
offer ofrecer

office   oficina (*f.*)

officer   agente (*m., f.*)

often   a menudo

Oh, goodness gracious! (God!)   ¡Ay, Dios mío!

oil   aceite (*m.*)

ointment   ungüento (*m.*)

okay   bueno

old   viejo(a), anciano(a)

older   mayor

oldest   el (la) mayor

on   en, a, (*by way of*) por, sobre; (*a light*)
   encendido(a), prendido(a)
   — **a bike**   en bicicleta
   — **becoming (turning) . . . years old**   al
      cumplir... años
   — **foot**   a pie
   — **(one's) side**   de lado
   — **the sides**   a los costados
   — **time**   a tiempo
   — **time payments**   a plazos
   — **top of**   sobre
   — **vacation**   de vacaciones

once again   otra vez

one   uno(a)
   — **hundred percent**   cien(to) por ciento
   — **-eyed**   tuerto(a)
   — **-handed**   manco(a)
   — **-legged**   cojo(a)
   the — who   el (la) que

only   (*adv.*) solamente, sólo; (*adj.*) único(a)
   the — thing   lo único

open   abrir; abierto(a)

opium   opio (*m.*)

opportunity   oportunidad (*f.*)

opposite opuesto(a)
  in the — direction en sentido contrario
option opción (*f.*)
or o
order ordenar; orden (de detención) (*f.*), permiso (de detención) (*m.*)
organization organización (*f.*)
organize organizar
original original
originate provenir
orthopedic ortopédico(a)
other otro(a)
  the others los (las) demás (*m., f.*); los (las) otros(as) (*m., f.*)
our nuestro(a), nuestros(as)
out (*light*) apagado(a)
  — on bail en libertad bajo fianza
  — on one's own recognizance en libertad bajo palabra
  — of order descompuesto(a)
outpatient paciente externo(a) (*m., f.*)
outside fuera
oven horno (*m.*)
over al dorso
over there para allá
overdose sobredosis (*f.*)
owe deber
own propio(a); poseer
  — a house tener casa propia
owner dueño(a) (*m., f.*)

P

pacifier chupete (*m.*), chupón (*m.*) (*Méx.*), tete (*m.*) (*Cuba*), bobo (*m.*) (*Puerto Rico*)

page página (*f.*)

paid (for) pagado(a)

pain dolor (*m.*)
— **killer** calmante (*m.*)

paint pintura (*f.*)

pal compañero(a) (*m., f.*)

pale pálido(a)

pants pantalón (*m.*), pantalones (*m. pl.*)

paper papel (*m.*)

paralyzed paralítico(a)

paramedic paramédico(a) (*m., f.*)

pardon perdón (*m.*); perdonar
— **me** perdón

parent helpline línea de ayuda a los padres (*f.*)

parents padres (*m. pl.*)

park parque (*m.*)

parked estacionado(a)

parking lot zona de estacionamiento (*f.*)

parochial parroquial

part parte (*f.*)

participate participar

party fiesta (*f.*)

pass (*a car*) pasar, rebasar (*Méx.*)
— **away** fallecer
do not — no pasar; no rebasar (*Méx.*)

passbook libreta de ahorros (*f.*)

passenger pasajero(a) (*m., f.*)

passport pasaporte (*m.*)

pastor pastor(a) (*m., f.*)

patience paciencia (*f.*)

patrol patrulla (*f.*)
  — **car** carro patrullero (*m.*)
pawn empeñar
pay pagar
  — **attention** (**to**) hacer caso (a), prestar
    atención (a)
  — **in installments** pagar a plazos
payment pago (*m.*)
pearl perla (*f.*)
  cultured — perla de cultivo (*f.*)
pedestrian peatón(ona) (*m., f.*)
pediatrician pediatra (*m., f.*)
penalty pena (*f.*), penalidad (*f.*)
pencil lápiz (*m.*)
penetration penetración (*f.*)
pension pensión (*f.*)
people gente (*f.*)
per day (**week**) por día (semana)
percent por ciento (*m.*)
perfect perfecto(a)
perform realizar
perhaps a lo mejor, quizá(s), tal vez
permanent permanente
permission permiso (*m.*)
permitted permitido(a)
perpetrate cometer
person persona (*f.*)
  in — en persona
personal personal
  — **data** dato personal (*m.*)
personally en persona
personnel personal (*m.*)
pharmacy farmacia (*f.*), botica (*f.*)
phone teléfono (*m.*); llamar por teléfono

by — por teléfono
on the — por teléfono
— call llamada telefónica (*f.*)
— number número de teléfono (*m.*)
photocopy copia fotostática (*f.*), fotocopia (*f.*)
photograph fotografía (*f.*); retratar
physical físico(a)
— therapy terapia física (*f.*)
pick up recoger
picklock llave falsa (*f.*), ganzúa (*f.*)
pierced atravesado(a)
pill píldora (*f.*), pastilla (*f.*)
pillow almohada (*f.*)
pimple grano (*m.*)
pinstriped a rayas
pint pinta (*f.*)
pistol pistola (*f.*)
place lugar (*m.*); colocar
— of birth lugar de nacimiento (*m.*)
to — nearby arrimar
plaid a cuadros
plan (to do something) pensar (e:ie) (+ *inf.*)
play jugar (u:ue)
— with fire jugar con fuego
please por favor
pneumonia pulmonía (*f.*), neumonía (*f.*)
pocket bolsillo (*m.*)
point (a gun) apuntar
poison (oneself) envenenar(se); veneno (*m.*)
police (*force*) policía (*f.*); (*officer*) policía (*m., f.*),
    agente de policía (*m., f.*)
— station comisaría (*f.*), estación de policía
    (*f.*), jefatura de policía (*f.*)
policy póliza (*f.*)

polka dot   de lunares
poor   pobre
porch   portal (*m.*)
pornographic   pornográfico(a)
portly   grueso(a)
position   posición (*f.*), cargo (*m.*)
possibility   posibilidad (*f.*)
possible   posible
possibly   posiblemente
post office   estación de correos (*f.*), oficina de
   correos (*f.*)
   — box   apartado postal (*m.*)
postal   postal
pound   libra (*f.*)
practice   practicar
prank   travesura (*f.*)
precaution   precaución (*f.*)
prefer   preferir (e:ie)
pregnancy   embarazo (*m.*)
pregnant   embarazada
preliminary   preliminar
premium   prima (*f.*)
prepare   preparar(se)
prescribe   recetar
prescribed   recetado(a)
prescription   receta (*f.*)
present   (*adj.*) actual, presente; presentar; (*gift*)
   regalo (*m.*)
pressure   presión (*f.*)
prevent   prevenir
preventive   preventivo(a)
previous   anterior
priest (Catholic)   padre (*m.*), cura (*m.*), sacerdote
   (*m.*)

principal (**at a school**) director(a) (de la escuela) (*m., f.*)

print estampado(a)

printing letra de molde (*f.*)

prison cárcel (*f.*), prisión (*f.*)

prisoner preso(a) (*m., f.*)

private privado(a)

  — **property** propiedad privada (*f.*)

probable probable

probation libertad condicional (*f.*)

problem problema (*m.*)

profession profesión (*f.*)

profit ganancia (*f.*)

program programa (*m.*)

prohibit prohibir

prohibited prohibido(a)

promise prometer

proof prueba (*f.*)

property propiedad (*f.*)

  — **tax** impuesto a (sobre) la propiedad (*m.*)

prosecutor fiscal (*m., f.*)

prostitute prostituto(a) (*m., f.*)

prostitution prostitución (*f.*)

protect proteger

protest protestar

Protestant protestante

provide proporcionar

provisional provisional

psychologist psicólogo(a) (*m., f.*)

public público(a)

  notary — notario(a) publico(a) (*m., f.*)

pull over (**a car**) arrimar

punch trompada (*f.*), puñetazo (*m.*)

punish castigar

purse cartera (*f.*), bolsa (*f.*), bolso (*m.*)
pus pus (*m.*)
push empujar
put poner, colocar
　— **away** guardado(a); guardar
　— **in one's mouth** meterse en la boca
　— **on** ponerse
　— **one's hands against the wall** poner las
　　manos en la pared
　— **out (a fire)** apagar
　— **to bed** acostar (o:ue)

Q

qualify calificar
quantity cantidad (*f.*)
quarter (three months) trimestre (*m.*), cuarto
　(*m.*)
　— **of an hour** cuarto de hora (*m.*)
question interrogar; pregunta (*f.*)
questioning interrogatorio (*m.*)
questionnaire cuestionario (*m.*)
quick(ly) rápido
quiet callado(a), quieto(a)
quite bastante

R

rabbi rabí (*m.*), rabino (*m.*)
race raza (*f.*)
railroad ferrocarril (*m.*)
　— **insurance** seguro ferroviario (*m.*)
rain llover; lluvia (*f.*)
raincoat impermeable (*m.*), capa da agua (*f.*)

raising (upbringing)   crianza (*f.*)

ransom   rescate (*m.*)

rape   violar; violación (*f.*)

rather   más bien, medio, bastante

razor   navaja (*f.*)

reach   llegar (a)

read   leer

ready   listo(a)

real   verdadero(a)

— **estate**   bienes raíces (*m. pl.*), bienes inmuebles (*m. pl.*)

realize   darse cuenta (de)

Really?   ¿De veras?

reason   porqué (*m.*)

receipt   recibo (*m.*), comprobante (*m.*)

receive   recibir

recent   reciente

recently   recientemente

recertification   recertificación (*f.*)

receptionist   recepcionista (*m., f.*)

recipient   recipiente (*m., f.*)

recite   recitar

recklessly   imprudentemente

recognize   reconocer

recommend   recomendar (e:ie)

reconciliation   reconciliación (*f.*)

record player   tocadiscos (*m.*)

recover   recobrar

red   rojo(a)

— **Cross**   Cruz Roja (*f.*)

— **-haired**   pelirrojo(a)

reevaluate   reevaluar

reformatory   reformatorio (*m.*)

refrigerator   refrigerador (*m.*), nevera (*f.*)

refund reembolso (*m.*)

refuse (to) negarse (e:ie) (a), rehusar

register matricularse, registrarse

registered registrado(a), matriculado(a)

registration registro (*m.*), registración (*f.*)
  (*Méx.*), matrícula (*f.*)

regret arrepentirse (e:ie)
  — **that . . .** sentir (e:ie) que

related relacionado(a)

relationship (in a family) parentesco (*m.*)

relative pariente(a) (*m., f.*)

relax calmarse

remain permanecer

remaining ones los (las) demás

remember recordar (o:ue), acordarse (o:ue) (de)

rent alquiler (*m.*), renta (*f.*)

repair reparación (*f.*)

report notificar, (*a crime*) denunciar, avisar de;
  (*of a crime*) denuncia (*f.*), reporte (*m.*), informe
  (*m.*)

represent representar

request pedir (e:i)

required requerido(a)

rescue rescatar

residence residencia (*f.*)

resident residente (*m., f.*)

residential residencial

resign renunciar

resist hacer resistencia

resisting arrest resistencia a la autoridad (*f.*)

respond responder

responsible responsable

rest resto (*m.*); descansar
  the — lo demás

restaurant restaurante (*m.*)
restless travieso(a), majadero(a), juguetón(ona)
retire jubilarse, retirarse
retired jubilado(a), pensionado(a), retirado(a)
retirement jubilación (*f.*), retiro (*m.*)
return regresar, volver (o:ue)
revenue ingreso (*m.*)
reverse reverso (*m.*)
review revisar; revisión (*f.*)
revolver revólver (*m.*)
rheumatism reumatismo (*m.*)
rich rico(a)
rifle rifle (*m.*)
right (*law*) derecho (*m.*), (*direction*) derecha (*f.*)
  —? ¿verdad?
  — **away** en seguida, ahorita (*Méx.*)
  — **-hand side** derecha (*f.*)
  — **now** ahora mismo
  That's —. Es cierto.
  to the — a la derecha
ring anillo (*m.*)
  — **finger** (dedo) anular (*m.*)
risk riesgo (*m.*)
road camino (*m.*)
rob robar
robbery robo (*m.*)
rock (*coll. for* **crack cocaine**) piedra (*f.*)
roof techo (*m.*)
room cuarto (*m.*), habitación (*f.*)
  — **and board** el alojamiento y las comidas
    (*m.*)
rope soga (*f.*)
routinely de rutina
rug alfombra (*f.*)

rule reglamento (*m.*)
rump nalga (*f.*)
run correr
   — **away** escaparse, fugarse
   — **into** chocar

S

safe seguro(a)
safety seguridad (*f.*)
   — **belt** cinturón de seguridad (*m.*)
   — **(bike) helmet** casco de seguridad (*m.*)
   — **cap (cover)** tapa de seguridad (*f.*)
salary sueldo (*m.*), salario (*m.*)
same mismo(a)
   the — as before el (la) mismo(a) de antes
      (*m., f.*)
sandal sandalia (*f.*)
save guardar, salvar
saved guardado(a)
savings account cuenta de ahorros (*f.*)
say decir (e:i)
scar cicatriz (*f.*)
scarf bufanda (*f.*)
schedule horario (*m.*)
scholarship beca (*f.*)
school escuela (*f.*)
   — **crossing** cruce de niños (*m.*)
scissors tijeras (*f. pl.*)
scratch rasguño (*m.*)
scream gritar
sealed sellado(a)
seat asiento (*m.*)
second segundo(a)

secondary school (junior and high school) escuela secundaria (*f.*)

secret secreto(a)

section sección (*f.*), división (*f.*)

security deposit depósito de seguridad (*m.*)

sedative calmante (*m.*), sedante (*m.*), sedativo (*m.*)

see ver

— **you later.** Hasta luego.

— **you tomorrow.** Hasta mañana.

seem parecer

seen visto(a)

self-defense: in — en defensa propia

self-employed: to be — trabajar por su cuenta, trabajar por cuenta propia

sell vender

semester semestre (*m.*)

semiautomatic semiautomático(a)

semiprivate semiprivado(a)

send mandar, enviar

sentence dictar sentencia, sentenciar; sentencia (*f.*), condena (*f.*)

sentimental sentimental

separate separar

separation separación (*f.*)

sergeant sargento (*m., f.*)

serial number número de serie (*m.*)

series serie (*f.*)

serious grave, serio(a)

servant sirviente (*m., f.*)

serve servir (e:i)

service servicio (*m.*)

— **station** estación de servicio (*f.*), gasolinera (*f.*)

set on fire   dar fuego, pegar fuego, incendiar
several   varios(as)
sex   sexo (*m.*)
sexual   sexual
   — abuse   abuso sexual (*m.*)
   — relations   relaciones sexuales (*f. pl.*)
shaded   sombreado(a)
shake   temblar (e:ie)
share (of stock)   acción (*f.*)
shave   afeitarse
shirt   camisa (*f.*)
shiver   temblar (e:ie)
shock absorber   amortiguador de choque (*m.*)
shoe   zapato (*m.*)
shoelace   cordón (del zapato) (*m.*)
shoot   disparar, tirar, dar un tiro, dar un balazo,
   pegar un tiro, pegar un balazo
   — up   pullar (*coll.*) (*Caribe*)
short   (*in height*) bajo(a), bajito(a) (*Cuba*),
   chaparro(a) (*Méx.*); (*in length*) corto(a); (*in
   duration*) breve
shorts   shorts (*m. pl.*)
short-sleeved   de mangas cortas
shot   balazo (*m.*), tiro (*m.*)
shotgun   escopeta (*f.*)
should (do something)   deber (+ *inf.*)
shoulder   hombro (*m.*)
shout   gritar
show   mostrar (o:ue), enseñar
shower   ducharse
Shut up!   ¡Cállese!
sick   enfermo(a)
sickness   enfermedad (*f.*)
side   lado (*m.*)

sidewalk acera (*f.*), banqueta (*f.*) (*Méx.*)

sign firmar

signature firma (*f.*)

silent callado(a)

silver plata (*f.*)

silverware cubiertos (*m. pl.*)

simply simplemente

since desde

sincerely sinceramente

single soltero(a)

sir señor (Sr.) (*m.*)

sister hermana (*f.*)

   — **-in-law** cuñada (*f.*)

sit sentarse (e:ie)

   — **(stay) still** quedarse quieto(a)

   — **down.** Siéntese.

situation situación (*f.*)

sixth sexto(a)

size tamaño (*m.*)

skeleton key llave falsa (*f.*), ganzúa (*f.*)

skin piel (*f.*)

skinny flaco(a)

skirt falda (*f.*)

slap bofetada (*f.*), galleta (*f.*) (*Cuba y Puerto Rico*)

   — **on the buttocks** nalgada (*f.*)

sleep dormir (o:ue)

sleeveless sin mangas

slip resbalar

slow despacio

slowly despacio

small pequeño(a)

   — **truck** camioncito (*m.*)

smell olor (*m.*)
  — **of** olor a
smoke humo (*m.*); fumar
smuggle contrabandear
smuggling contrabando (*m.*)
snow nevar (e:ie); nieve (*f.*)
so así que, así, tan, por lo tanto
  — **long** tanto tiempo
  — **long!** Hasta luego.
  — **many** tantos(as)
  — **that** de modo que, para que
soap jabón (*m.*)
sobriety test prueba del alcohol (*f.*)
social social
  — **Security** Seguro Social (*m.*)
  — **Security card** tarjeta de Seguro Social (*f.*)
  — **services** asistencia social (*f.*)
  — **Welfare Department** Departamento de
    Bienestar Social (*m.*)
  — **worker** trabajador(a) social (*m., f.*)
  — **worker who makes home
    visits** visitador(a) social (*m., f.*)
socket tomacorrientes (*m. sing.*), enchufe (*m.*)
socks calcetines (*m. pl.*), medias de hombre (*f. pl.*), tobilleras (*f. pl.*) (*Méx.*)
sofa sofá (*m.*)
solicit solicitar
solve resolver (o:ue)
some algún, alguno(a), unos(as)
somebody alguien
someone alguien
  — **else** otra persona (*f.*)
something algo
sometimes a veces

son hijo (*m.*)
   — **-in-law** yerno (*m.*)
sonogram sonograma (*m.*)
soon pronto
sorry: I'm —. Lo siento.
source of income fuente de ingreso (*f.*)
south sur (*m.*)
southeast sureste (*m.*)
southwest suroeste (*m.*)
Spanish (language) español (*m.*)
spanking paliza (*f.*), nalgada (*f.*)
sparkplug bujía (*f.*)
speak hablar
special especial
specialist especialista (*m., f.*)
specify especificar
speech impediment dificultad del habla (*f.*)
speed velocidad (*f.*); (*drugs*) clavo (*m.*) (*coll.*)
   — **limit** límite de velocidad (*m.*), velocidad
     máxima (*f.*)
spell deletrear
spend (*money*) gastar; (*time*) pasar
sports car carro deportivo (*m.*)
spot mancha (*f.*)
spread extender (e:ie)
   — **one's feet** separar los pies
spreadeagle abrir las piernas y los brazos
spring primavera (*f.*)
   — **break** descanso de primavera (*m.*),
     vacaciones de primavera (*f. pl.*)
stab dar una puñalada
staff personal (*m.*)
stairs escalera (*f.*)

stand pararse
  — **up!** ¡Póngase de pie!
standing parado(a)
start iniciar; (*a car*) arrancar
starter arranque (*m.*), motor de arranque (*m.*)
starting with a partir de
state estado (*m.*); (*adj.*) estatal
statue estatua (*f.*)
stay permanecer, quedarse
steal (from) robar, llevarse
steering wheel volante (*m.*), timón (*m.*) (*Cuba*)
stenographer taquígrafo(a) (*m., f.*)
step paso (*m.*)
stepbrother hermanastro (*m.*)
stepdaughter hijastra (*f.*)
stepfather padrastro (*m.*)
stepmother madrastra (*f.*)
stepsister hermanastra (*f.*)
stepson hijastro (*m.*)
still (*adv.*) todavía; (*adj.*) quieto(a)
stock acción (*f.*)
stockings medias (*f. pl.*)
stolen robado(a)
stomach estómago (*m.*)
stone piedra (*f.*)
stop suspender, detener, parar
  —! ¡Alto!, ¡Párese!, ¡Pare!
  — **(doing something)** dejar de (+ *inf.*)
  — **line** línea de parada (*f.*)
  — **mail (newspaper) delivery** suspender la
    entrega del correo (del periódico)
storage almacenaje (*m.*)
store tienda (*f.*)
stove fogón (*m.*), cocina (*f.*)

straight (*hair*) lacio(a)

   to go — ahead seguir (e:i) derecho

strange (unknown) extraño(a)

stranger persona extraña (*f.*), extraño(a) (*m., f.*), desconocido(a) (*m., f.*)

street calle (*f.*)

stretch out extender (e:ie)

stretcher camilla (*f.*)

strike pegar, golpear, dar golpes

stroke derrame cerebral (*m.*), embolia (*f.*)

struggle luchar

student estudiante (*m., f.*)

   — visa visa de estudiante (*f.*)

study estudiar

   — a language tomar un idioma

stutter tartamudear

stutterer tartamudo(a) (*m., f.*)

submit (oneself) to someterse a

subscription suscripción (*f.*)

subsidy subvención (*f.*), subsidio (*m.*)

succeed in (doing something) llegar a (+ *inf.*)

such a thing tal cosa

sue demandar

sufficient suficiente

suffocate asfixiar

suggest sugerir (e:ie)

summer verano (*m.*)

sun sol (*m.*)

supermarket mercado (*m.*), supermercado (*m.*)

supervisor supervisor(a) (*m., f.*)

supplemental suplementario(a)

support (oneself) apoyo (*m.*); mantener(se) (e:ie)

supreme court tribunal supremo (*m.*)

sure seguro(a)

Sure! ¡Cómo no!
surgeon cirujano(a) (*m., f.*)
surname apellido (*m.*)
suspect sospechar
suspicion sospecha (*f.*)
suspicious sospechoso(a)
swear jurar
sweater suéter (*m.*)
swimming pool piscina (*f.*), alberca (*f.*) (*Méx.*)
swindle estafar; estafa (*f.*)
switchblade navaja (*f.*)
symptom síntoma (*m.*)
synagogue sinagoga (*f.*)
syphilis sífilis (*f.*)
syrup jarabe (*m.*)
system sistema (*m.*)

T

table mesa (*f.*)
take llevar, tomar, agarrar, coger
   — **a seat** tomar asiento
   — **a step** dar un paso
   — **away** quitar
   — **care of** atender (e:ie), cuidar
   — **drugs** endrogarse
   — **measures** tomar medidas
   — **note** anotar
   — **off (clothing)** quitarse
   — **out** sacar
   — **part** participar
   — **(someone or something**
    somewhere) llevar
   — **(time)** demorar

talk hablar, conversar
tall alto(a)
tank tanque (*m.*)
tape recorder grabadora (*f.*)
tattoo tatuaje (*m.*)
tax impuesto (*m.*)
taxpayer contribuyente (*m., f.*)
teacher maestro(a) (*m., f.*)
technician técnico(a) (*m., f.*)
teenager adolescente (*m., f.*), jovencito(a) (*m., f.*)
telephone teléfono (*m.*)
  — **book** guía telefónica (*f.*), guía de teléfonos
    (*f.*), directorio telefónico (*m.*)
  — **number** número de teléfono (*m.*)
  — **operator** telefonista (*m., f.*)
television (set) televisor (*m.*)
tell decir (e:i), contar (o:ue), informar
  — **a lie** mentir (e:ie)
temperature temperatura (*f.*)
temple sinagoga (*f.*)
temporary temporal
tennis shoe zapato de tenis (*m.*)
tenth décimo(a)
tequila tequila (*f.*)
term plazo (*m.*); término (*m.*)
terrace terraza (*f.*)
terrible terrible
terrified aterrorizado(a)
test análisis (*m.*), prueba (*f.*)
tetanus shot inyección antitetánica (*f.*)
textbook libro de texto (*m.*)
thank agradecer
  — **you (very much).** (Muchas) Gracias.
  — **goodness!** ¡Qué bueno!, menos mal

that que, ese(a), aquel, aquello(a); eso
   — **is to say . . .** Es decir...
   — **one** ése(a)
   — **way** así
   —**'s all.** Eso es todo.
   —**'s fine.** Está bien.
   —**'s great!** ¡Qué bueno!
   —**'s why** por eso
their su(s)
then entonces, luego
there para allá, allá, allí, ahí
   — **are (+ *number*) of us.** Somos (+ *number*).
   — **is (are)** hay
   — **is going to be** va a haber
   — **was (were)** había, hubo
therefore por lo tanto
thermometer termómetro (*m.*)
these estos(as)
thief ladrón(ona) (*m., f.*)
thin delgado(a), flaco(a)
thing cosa (*f.*), artículo (*m.*)
think creer, pensar (e:ie)
   not — so creer que no
   — **about that** pensar (e:ie) en eso
   — **so** creer que sí
third tercero(a)
this este(a)
   — **one** éste(a) (*m., f.*)
   — **time** esta vez
   — **very day** hoy mismo
those aquéllos(as) (*m., f.*)
threat amenaza (*f.*)
threaten amenazar
throat garganta (*f.*)

through por
throw echar
  — away tirar
thumb pulgar (*m.*)
ticket multa (*f.*)
tie corbata (*f.*)
tile roof techo de tejas (*m.*)
tilt one's head back echar la cabeza hacia
  atrás
time hora (*f.*), tiempo (*m.*), vez (*f.*)
  just in — a tiempo
  on — a tiempo
tip punta (*f.*)
tire llanta (*f.*), goma (*f.*) (*Cuba*), neumático (*m.*)
tired cansado(a)
tissues pañuelos de papel (*m. pl.*)
title título (*m.*)
to a, hacia, para
  — (at) the al, del
  — the left (right) a la izquierda (derecha)
today hoy
  —'s date fecha de hoy (*f.*)
toe dedo del pie (*m.*)
together juntos(as)
tomorrow mañana
  the day after — pasado mañana (*m.*)
tongue lengua (*f.*)
tonight esta noche
too también
  — much demasiado(a)
tooth diente (*m.*)
top quality de primera calidad
total total
totally totalmente

touch tocar
toward hacia
town pueblo (*m.*)
toy juguete (*m.*)
   — **store** juguetería (*f.*)
trade oficio (*m.*)
traffic tráfico (*m.*), tránsito (*m.*)
  slow — tráfico lento (*m.*), tránsito lento (*m.*)
  — **light** semáforo (*m.*)
  — **sign** señal de tránsito (*f.*)
  — **violation** infracción de tránsito (*f.*)
trained entrenado(a)
training entrenamiento (*m.*), capacitación (*f.*)
tranquilizer sedante (*m.*)
transfusion transfusión (*f.*)
transgression of law delito (*m.*)
translator traductor(a) (*m., f.*)
transportation transportación (*f.*)
trash basura (*f.*)
treat tratar
treatment tratamiento (*m.*)
tremble temblar (e:ie)
trespassing: no — prohibido pasar
trial juicio (*m.*)
trim bushes (trees) podar arbustos (árboles)
trimester trimestre (*m.*)
trip viaje (*m.*)
trousers pantalón (*m.*), pantalones (*m. pl.*)
truck camión (*m.*)
true verdadero(a)
  —? ¿verdad?
trunk (of a car) maletero (*m.*), cajuela (*f.*) (*Méx.*),
  baúl (*m.*) (*Puerto Rico*), portaequipajes (*m.*)
truth verdad (*f.*)

try   tratar (de)
T-shirt   camiseta (*f.*)
tuberculosis   tuberculosis (*f.*)
tumor   tumor (*m.*)
turn   doblar, ponerse
— **around**   darse vuelta, voltearse (*Méx.*), virarse
— **blue**   ponerse azul
— **off**   apagar
— **on (a light)**   prender, encender (e:ie)
— **over (something to someone)**   entregarle a
— **pale**   ponerse pálido(a)
— **red**   ponerse rojo(a)
— **signal**   indicador (*m.*)
— **to**   recurrir (a)
— **white**   ponerse blanco(a)
TV   televisor (*m.*)
tweezers   pinzas (*f. pl.*)
twice   dos veces
two-way traffic   doble circulación (*f.*), doble vía (*f.*)
type   clase (*f.*), tipo (*m.*); escribir a máquina

U

unable to work   incapacitado(a) para trabajar
uncle   tío (*m.*)
uncomfortable   incómodo(a)
under   debajo (de)
— **the influence (of)**   bajo los efectos (de)
undercover police   policía secreta (*f.*)
underneath   debajo de
understand   entender (e:ie), comprender

unfortunately   por desgracia, desgraciadamente
united   unido(a)
unless   a menos que
until   hasta, hasta que
  — recently   hasta hace poco
unusual   no usual
up to . . .   hasta el/la...
upholstery   tapicería (*f.*)
upset   disgustado(a)
up-to-date   al día
urgent   urgente
urgently   urgentemente
urine   orina (*f.*)
us   nosotros(as) (*m., f.*)
use   uso (*m.*); usar, utilizar
  can be used   puede usarse
  will be used   se usará
used   usado(a)
useful   útil
usual   usual
usually   generalmente

V

vacant   desocupado(a)
vacate   desocupar, desalojar
vacation   vacaciones (*f. pl.*), descanso (*m.*)
vaccinate   vacunar
vagina   vagina (*f.*)
valid   válido(a)
value   valor (*m.*)
vandalism   vandalismo (*m.*)
vehicle   vehículo (*m.*)
venereal   venéreo(a)

— **disease**   enfermedad venérea (*f.*)
verb   verbo (*m.*)
verdict   fallo (*m.*), veredicto (*m.*)
verification   verificación (*f.*)
verify   verificar
very   muy
   — **much**   muchísimo(a)
   (Not) — well.   (No) Muy bien.
veterinary   veterinario(a) (*m., f.*)
victim   víctima (*f.*)
video camera   cámara de vídeo (*f.*), videocámara
   (*f.*)
videocassette recorder (VCR)   videocasetera
   (*f.*), videograbadora (*f.*)
violent   violento(a)
visible   visible
visit   visitar
visitation rights   derecho a visitar (*m.*)
visiting nurse   enfermero(a) visitador(a) (*m., f.*)
vocabulary   vocabulario (*m.*)
vocational   vocacional
   — **training**   reorientación vocacional (*f.*)
voluntarily   voluntariamente

W

waist   cintura (*f.*)
   — **-high**   a nivel de la cintura
wait   esperar
   — **on**   atender (e:ie)
waive   renunciar
wake (someone up)   despertar (e:ie)
   — **up**   despertarse (e:ie)
walk   andar, caminar

walker andador (*m.*)

wall pared (*f.*)

wallet cartera (*f.*), billetera (*f.*)

want desear, querer (e:ie)

warn avisar, hacer saber

warrant orden de detención (*f.*), permiso de detención (*m.*)

wart verruga (*f.*)

washcloth toallita (*f.*)

waste perder (e:ie)

watch reloj (*m.*); mirar

watching mirando

water agua (*f.* but **el agua**)

  — **pump** bomba de agua (*f.*)

watering riego (*m.*)

way forma (*f.*), manera (*f.*)

  It is not that —. No es así.

weapon arma (*f.* but **el arma**)

wear llevar, llevar puesto(a), tener puesto(a)

week semana (*f.*)

weekend fin de semana (*m.*)

weekly (*adj.*) semanal; (*adv.*) semanalmente, por semana

weigh pesar

weight peso (*m.*)

welcome: You're —. De nada., No hay de qué.

well bien

what lo que

what? ¿qué?, ¿cuál?

  — **can I do for you?** ¿En qué puedo servirle (ayudarle)?, ¿Qué se le ofrece?

  — **do you (does he/she) need?** ¿Qué necesita?

  — **else?** ¿Qué más?

    — for? ¿para qué?

    — time was (is) it? ¿Qué hora era (es)?

    —'s happening? ¿Qué pasa?

    —'s new? ¿Qué hay de nuevo?

    —'s wrong? ¿Qué tiene?

wheel rueda (*f.*)

wheelchair silla de ruedas (*f.*)

when cuando

when? ¿cuándo?

where? ¿dónde?

    to —? ¿adónde? (¿a dónde?)

whereabouts paradero (*m.*)

which? ¿cuál?

while mientras; rato (*m.*)

white blanco(a)

who? ¿quién?

whole: the — ... todo(a) el (la)...

whom? ¿quién?

whose cuyo(a)

why? ¿para qué?, ¿por qué?

widow viuda (*f.*)

widower viudo (*m.*)

wife esposa (*f.*), mujer (*f.*), señora (*f.*)

wig peluca (*f.*)

will voluntad (*f.*)

willing dispuesto(a)

window ventana (*f.*); (*in a car*) ventanilla (*f.*)

windshield parabrisas (*m.*)

    — wiper limpiaparabrisas (*m. sing.*)

wine vino (*m.*)

winter invierno (*m.*)

wish desear, querer (e:ie)

with con

    — (black) hair de pelo (negro)

— **(blue) eyes** de ojos (azules)
— **her** con ella, consigo
— **him** con él, consigo
— **me** conmigo
— **you** contigo (*informal*), consigo(a) (*form.*)
withdraw retirarse
within dentro de
— **reach** a su alcance
without sin
— **cost** gratis
— **fail** sin falta
witness testigo (*m., f.*)
woman mujer (*f.*)
wonderful maravilloso(a)
word palabra (*f.*)
work trabajar, trabajo (*m.*)
— **full-time** trabajar a tiempo completo
— **part-time** trabajar parte del tiempo, trabajar medio día
— **permit** permiso de trabajo (*m.*)
worker obrero(a) (*m., f.*), trabajador(a) (*m., f.*)
—**'s compensation** compensación obrera (*f.*)
working: not — descompuesto(a)
worried preocupado(a)
worry preocuparse
worse peor
wound herida (*f.*)
wrist muñeca (*f.*)
write escribir
— **down** anotar

X

X (*letter of alphabet*) equis (*f.*)

X-ray   radiografía (*f.*)

Y

yard   patio (*m.*)
year   año (*m.*)
yearly   (*adv.*) al año; (*adj.*) anual
yellow   amarillo(a)
yes   sí
yesterday   ayer
yet   todavía
young   joven
   — **boy (girl)**   chico(a) (*m., f.*), chamaco(a)
      (*m., f.*) (*Méx.*)
   — **lady**   señorita (*f.*)
   — **man (woman)**   joven (*m., f.*)
younger   menor
youngest   el (la) menor
You're welcome.   No hay de qué.
your   su (*form.*), tu (*informal*)
yours   suyo(a) (*form.*), tuyo(a) (*informal*)
yourself   sí mismo(a) (*form.*), tú mismo(a)
   (*informal*)

Z

zip code   zona postal (*f.*), código postal (*m.*)
   (*Méx.*)
zone   zona (*f.*)